GOSPEL SYMBOLS

finding THE CREATOR IN HIS CREATIONS

MARK A. SHIELDS

CFI
Springville, Utah

ISBN 13: 978-1-59955-269-9

Published by CFI, an imprint of Cedar Fort, Inc., 2373 W. 700 S., Springville, UT 84663
Distributed by Cedar Fort, Inc., www.cedarfort.com

LIBRARY OF CONGRESS CATALOGING-IN-PUBLICATION DATA

Shields, Mark A. (Mark Alan)
Gospel symbols : finding the creator in his creations / Mark A. Shields.
p. cm.
Includes bibliographical references.
ISBN 978-1-59955-269-9 (acid-free paper)
1. Christian art and symbolism. 2. Symbolism in the Bible. 3. Symbolism in the Book of Mormon. 4. Church of Jesus Christ of Latter-day Saints--Doctrines. I. Title.

BX8635.3.S55 2009
230'.9332--dc22

2009009974

Cover design by Angela D. Olsen
Cover design © 2010 by Lyle Mortimer
Edited and typeset by Heidi Doxey

Printed in the United States of America

10 9 8 7 6 5 4 3 2 1

Printed on acid-free paper

DEDICATED to Heidi, Kayla, Claire, Anna, and Robyn—May you always love the Savior and discover and rediscover Him each day in all of the lessons He has given us of His love, His power, and His plan.

ACKNOWLEDGMENTS

Special thanks to Doug Clark for his contributions to this work. Thank you also to Heidi Doxey, Jennifer Hughes, Jenny Christensen, Ruth Hyde, my wife Cami, and my father Gordon for their kind and generous help and encouragement. Thank you also to Professors Richard Draper, Kenneth Hamblin, and Donald Parry, who almost certainly will not remember the kind assistance and inspiration they provided years ago at BYU for this project. And last of all, special thanks to my dear friend and mission president Doug Holt for opening my eyes, my ears, my mind, and my heart to the wonderful world of gospel symbolism.

Also by Mark A. Shields

Your Endowment: Gain Greater Joy and Satisfaction in Your Temple Service

Table of Contents

Foreword

Our merciful Creator has woven into the very fabric of creation signs and symbols of His existence and love. "All things," the Book of Mormon emphasizes, "denote there is a God" (Alma 30:44) and "are the typifying of him" (2 Nephi 11:4).

Hence the Psalmist's assurance that "the heavens declare the glory of God" (Psalms 19:1). Or, as God Himself explains in latter-day revelation, "any man who hath seen any or the least of these"—referring to the earth, moon, sun, and stars—"hath seen God moving in his majesty and power" (D&C 88:47), for "he is above all things, and in all things, and is through all things, and is round about all things; and all things are by him, and of him, even God, forever and ever" (D&C 88:41).

Such universal evidence of the Creator remains intact even during times of apostasy, and stirs the souls of some of the greatest mortals, inviting them to pray and assuring them that answers await. The boy Abraham learned of the existence of the Creator by observing His creations, as did the boy Joseph Smith. The 1832 account of the First Vision tells that it was only after contemplating the cosmos and nature that Joseph became convinced there was a God to whom he could turn.

The heavens were opened and the gospel was restored, but God's magnificent works, even "all things," still invite us to learn more of Him and delve deeper into His goodness.

This book helps us do precisely that, offering a delightful exploration of the possible significance of such diverse "things" as the cosmos, light, and gravity; water, rocks, and trees; the sun, moon, and seasons; parts of the Mosaic law; and even the lives of several key prophets through the ages.

No mortal can fathom, let alone explain, the divine symbolism in "all things," but we are expected—for our own benefit and blessing—to zealously seek and ponder. Mark Shields has done so, and his insights deepen our appreciation for the power, majesty, and love of our Creator and Redeemer.

—Doug Clark

Doug Clark is the author of The Blessings of Abraham—Becoming a Zion People, *and* The Grand Design, *and the co-author of* Fathers and Sons in the Book of Mormon. *He is also the author of the foreword in Hugh Nibley's* Abraham in Egypt *and wrote the entry on Abraham in* The Encyclopedia of Mormonism *as well as numerous other articles published by FARMS and BYU Studies.*

Introduction

And behold, all things have their likeness, and all things are created and made to bear record of me, both things which are temporal, and things which are spiritual; things which are in the heavens above, and things which are on the earth, and things which are in the earth, and things which are under the earth, both above and beneath: all things bear record of me. (Moses 6:63)

All things which have been given of God from the beginning of the world, unto man, are the typifying of him. (2 Nephi 11:4)

Yea, even the earth and all things that are upon the face of it, yea, and its motion, yea, and also all the planets which move in their regular form do witness that there is a Supreme Creator. (Alma 30:44)

Finding Hidden Treasures

I have always been a fan of action adventure movies. Like most people my age, I grew up loving Indiana Jones. More recently, I've enjoyed the National Treasure movies. The heroes in these movies follow strings of clues, deciphering complex codes and riddles and beating the evil opposition to find the hidden and sacred treasures. Adding to the adventure, the heroes' goal isn't just to get the lost treasure; their goal is also to keep the treasure out of evil hands that would misuse the power that comes with the treasure. Fortunately, in all the movies I've seen, the heroes have succeeded in following all the clues and keeping the sacred or priceless treasures out of the wrong hands.

The process of finding hidden, sacred treasures through gospel symbolism is actually somewhat similar. As the scriptures testify, all things created by the hand of the Lord bear witness of Him or typify Him. That means that all creations are evidence of their Creator and all things teach of their Creator. So, the clues to a profound treasure of gospel knowledge are right before us in our everyday world.

We have been assured that the symbols and hidden treasures of knowledge around us are ours for the finding. Still, many people in the world will see a sunrise, a tree, a piece of bread, or countless other things and fail to make any connection between the object and its Creator. At the same time, those who truly seek to confess the hand of the Lord in all things (see D&C 59:21) will dig more deeply in search of a hidden lesson with a more profound meaning. Through an understanding of symbols, these people will indeed find those treasures—if they walk in obedience to the commandments (see D&C 89:18–19).

Symbolism works to keep the treasures hidden from those who are spiritually unprepared for them, those who, like the fictional antagonists in the movies, might not know how to use the knowledge properly. At the same time, symbolism deeply rewards the earnest seeker of truth who digs more deeply to discover such treasures.

However, the analogy between movie characters seeking treasure and scripture readers seeking hidden sacred treasures is less than perfect. There are distinct differences between the fictitious and the true seekers of hidden treasures. In the movies, the fictional treasure hunters, whether they're "good" or "evil," find some kind of instant spiritual power just by applying their knowledge to find the sacred treasure. For example, Indiana Jones is able to navigate his way past the "judgments of God" by knowing certain things, such as how to spell the name of God in a certain language or by remembering to duck, as a penitent man would bow, to avoid decapitation.

While these tidbits of knowledge do influence Indy's actions to some extent (such as taking the right footsteps and knowing to duck), these bits of trivial knowledge hardly govern his everyday life.

In contrast, we will not be saved or otherwise be able to stand in the presence of God by virtue of something we know, no matter how great or profound it may be. No scriptural insight or formula is enough by itself to bring salvation to anyone. There is no secret code or password that will allow you to take a shortcut into the Lord's presence. It takes more than knowledge; it takes intelligence.

Knowledge vs. Intelligence

The cardinal rule in understanding the hidden treasures that come from gospel symbolism is the realization that the glory of God is intelligence, not knowledge (see D&C 93:36). Knowledge may be the glory of man, but intelligence is the glory of God. Intelligence is "knowledge made alive and useful."[1] It is possible to gain great knowledge by studying symbolism and learning the application of symbols in the scriptures. But again, this leads to knowledge, not intelligence. Knowledge may be glorious, but it is not the glory of God. Knowledge that is acted on becomes intelligence, and that is the glory of God.

This true enlightenment—intelligence or light and truth—is gained only by the Holy Ghost. And the only way to have the Holy Ghost with us is by walking in obedience to the commandments of God (see D&C 93:28; 89:18–19). So true enlightenment comes after exercising faith, repenting, and being baptized (see Article of Faith 4). It comes from making sacred covenants and then keeping those covenants each day of our lives (see D&C 20:77, 79). It comes from renewing those covenants regularly. It comes from always remembering the Lord and His sacrifice.

As President Joseph Fielding Smith taught, "Now the Lord would give us gifts. He will quicken our minds. He will give us knowledge that will be so deeply rooted in our souls that [it] can never be rooted out, if we will just seek for the light and the understanding which is promised to us, and which we can receive if we will only be true and faithful to every covenant and obligation pertaining to the gospel of Jesus Christ."[2]

In other words, intelligence comes not just from knowing but also from understanding, appreciating, and living accordingly.

The purpose of this book is to help you unfold new levels of understanding and find the hidden treasures of the gospel that come from recognizing the Creator in His creations. When we understand that through symbolism all things bear witness of Christ, we are then invited to seek for and find hidden treasures of knowledge, and then apply them to the way we live. That leads to intelligence, not just knowledge.

To be sure, the purpose behind gospel symbolism is certainly not to create any shortcuts to heaven by learning secret facts or gaining some inside information. As I said before, there are no shortcuts to heaven. Likewise, gospel symbolism doesn't exist just so you can be impressed with an interesting insight and move on in life unaffected by the insight. Gospel symbols exist to teach gospel truths in ways that mere words cannot convey. This kind of learning is meant to shape who you are, not just what you know. And this is the kind of learning that leads to intelligence.

Learning in a Most Unusual Way

A vision recounted by Elder David B. Haight illustrates the kind of understanding that can come from gospel symbolism. Elder Haight had suffered a serious health crisis that left him unconscious and hospitalized for several days. During that time of unconsciousness, Elder Haight was given a marvelous vision of the Savior's earthly ministry. He "was shown a panoramic view of [Jesus'] earthly ministry: His baptism, His teaching, His healing the sick and lame, the mock trial, His crucifixion, His Resurrection and ascension."[3] Elder Haight was not speaking of gospel symbolism when he shared his vision with the Church at general conference, but the principle holds true nonetheless because both Elder Haight's vision and gospel symbolism testify of the same subject: the Savior and His Atonement.

Elder Haight testified of the effect that this vision had on him: "I witness to you that He is Jesus the Christ, the Son of God, Savior to all, Redeemer of all mankind, Bestower of infinite love, mercy, and forgiveness, the Light and Life of the world. I knew this truth before—I had never doubted nor wondered. But now I knew, because of the impressions of the Spirit upon my heart and soul, these divine truths in a most unusual way."[4]

At the time he received this vision, Elder Haight had been an apostle—a special witness of the Savior—for close to thirteen years. During his remarkable life, he had surely received other witnesses of the Lord Jesus Christ that were too sacred to share. However, with this vision and by the power of the Holy Ghost, he learned "these divine truths in a most unusual way."

This is precisely the kind of effect that gospel symbolism can have on the mind and heart of a faithful seeker of truth. Anyone attempting to gain gospel insights through symbolism must first have a testimony. Building on top of that testimony, layers of "divine truths" will be added "in a most unusual way" for those who sincerely seek that understanding.

For example, we may understand the ordinance of baptism as restored in the last days, but understanding the symbolism of baptism as taught through the Exodus story brings a deeper, more "unusual" understanding of the experience. By looking more deeply at this symbolic example, we see, among other things, that the Lord parted the waters to separate His covenant people from their worldly enemies (see Exodus 14:21–22). We see that the Lord placed a pillar of fire and a cloud of darkness between Israel and the armies of their adversary, but this protection was not indefinite or permanent: the children of Israel still had to actively cross the water (see Exodus 14:20–25).

These depictions are typical of the blessings and opposition that accompany missionary work and baptism. They also represent a deeper understanding of an essential gospel ordinance. They are a hidden treasure and a "more unusual" understanding of something we already know and understand—baptism.

The Lord promises us that we will find Him if we seek Him. At the same time, He promises to open doors to us if we knock (see D&C 88:63). To be sure, gospel symbolism requires us both to seek and to knock. To find these treasures, we have to look beyond what first meets the eye, and we have to ask continually for the Lord's spirit in order to understand the hidden lessons. But we are promised great blessings of divine truth if we do seek and knock. If this book helps you in any way as you go through that process, it is a success.

An Introduction to Symbolism

In gospel symbolism, the Lord uses physical or temporal objects to teach spiritual or eternal lessons. The Lord has taught, "by the power of my Spirit created I them; yea, all things both spiritual and temporal—First spiritual, secondly temporal, which is the beginning of my work; and again, first temporal, and secondly spiritual, which is the last of my work" (D&C 29:31–2). In a great revelation to Moses, He reiterates this truth. "For I, the Lord God, created all things of which I have spoken, spiritually, before they were naturally upon the face of the earth" (Moses 3:5).

On that same note, "All symbols have a dual meaning—The exoteric, or material, is given to the curious, while the esoteric, or spiritual is only to be found by the sincere seeker after truth."[5] In other words, the physical world can teach us spiritual truths—if we sincerely seek the spiritual from the physical.

"Wherefore, verily I say unto you that all things unto me are spiritual, and not at any time have I given unto you a law which was temporal; neither any man, nor the children of men; neither Adam, your father, whom I created" (D&C 29:34). Along these same lines, the Savior taught, "If I have told you earthly things, and ye believe not, how shall ye believe, if I tell you of heavenly things?" (John 3:12). Here again is the underlying theme of gospel symbolism: The Lord uses the temporal to teach us of the eternal.

A perfect example of the physical being used to teach us the spiritual is found in the Book of Mormon account of the people of Ammon. After becoming converted to the gospel of Jesus Christ, they were so spiritually committed that they buried their weapons of war deep in the earth (see Alma 23, 24). This physical act symbolized a deep and abiding spiritual commitment to abandon their sins and former life of bloodshed. Their commitment to their covenant was so deep that they allowed themselves to be killed rather than break their covenant. This physical commitment brought about great spiritual blessings to their people, as other Lamanites were converted by their example.

Later, the next generation of this people also displayed valiant courage and commitment to righteousness. While they had not made the specific covenant to bury their weapons of war, they were committed to the cause of righteousness and fought to protect their loved ones. When these valiant young warriors returned from battle, every one of them had been injured, some severely. But through what was likely hundreds if not thousands of miracles, not one of them died. (see Alma 57:25). This miraculous preservation was attributed to their faith, the power of God (see Alma 57:26–27), their exact and unfailing obedience (see Alma 57:21), and the fact that they heeded the teachings of their mothers (see Alma 56:47–48).

As a physical occurrence, this story is nothing less than miraculous. But it is much more than a physical lesson. It is a spiritual lesson that beautifully illustrates the power of faith, covenants, and obedience. Likely few of us will be called on to die physically in order to honor our covenants. However, when a person enters into those covenants, the act does represent the symbolic death of his old self, the natural man.

Likewise, in a spiritual sense, we will all be wounded while in mortality, just as all the stripling warriors were wounded in battle. We will all sin as natural men, and some of those sins may be grave, costing a great deal of blood. While physical death is inevitable either on the battlefield or off it, spiritual death is completely avoidable if we are true and faithful to our covenants, as the warriors were. All of God's children can avoid an eternal spiritual death through obedience to the laws and ordinances of the gospel.

The account of the people of Ammon is a physical embodiment of great spiritual truths. Consider also the Old Testament story of Samson. We know Samson for his affiliation with Delilah, his long hair, his superhuman strength, and how he lost that strength when his hair was cut (see Judges 13–16). It may be easy to dismiss this as an intriguing Old Testament story, but there are actually great spiritual truths within the physical story.

You see, Samson's story begins before he was born. After she had endured years of barrenness, Samson's mother conversed with an angel (see Judges 13:2–4). The angel gave her some specific charges. He told her not to drink wine or any strong drink and not to eat any unclean thing (see Judges 13:4). After conveying these commandments, Samson's mother was then promised that she would conceive and bear a son (see Judges 13:5).

When a commandment is given and a specific blessing is promised if that commandment is kept, it is called a covenant. So as part of this covenant, Samson's mother was also charged not to let a razor touch Samson's head so that the child could "be a Nazarite unto God from the womb; and he shall begin to deliver Israel out of the hands of the Philistines" (Judges 13:5).

Apparently, Samson's parents taught him well about this covenant, as he later explained it to Delilah (see Judges 16:17). And we know that Delilah then told the Philistines of the importance of Samson's hair and that Samson's strength left him when his hair was cut (see Judges 16:18–19).

Contrary to what many might believe, this is not a fanciful tale or a lesson in grooming. In fact, it's not a physical lesson at all. It is a lesson about covenants. I don't know that there was anything particularly special about Samson's hair, other than the fact that the Lord had chosen it as a token of a great and powerful covenant. As long as the covenant (i.e., Samson's hair) was kept intact, the promised blessing (great strength) remained intact as well. When Samson unwittingly divulged and then lost the token of the covenant, "the Lord was departed from him" (Judges 16:20), and his remarkable strength left him.

We can dwell on the physical aspects of this story, but the lesson the Lord wants to teach us is about the power and importance of making and keeping covenants. This is a spiritual lesson that in this case happens to be conveyed through physical media—hair and human strength. As the Lord has pronounced, there are countless spiritual and eternal lessons to be learned from the physical and temporal world around us.

Noticing the physical or "exoteric" side of things is inevitable because we live in a physical world and think in terms of physical things. But with effort we can learn the eternal or "esoteric" from the temporal and physical. In many cases, the physical example is a remarkable parallel to the spiritual principle, as with the accounts of the people of Ammon and Samson. Our challenge is to find the spiritual or eternal principles in the physical world and follow them.

An understanding of symbols and types also brings a new light to the Master's words: "And this is life eternal, that they might know thee the only true God, and Jesus Christ, whom thou hast sent" (John 17:3). When we come to see how earthly creations such as water and rocks can testify of Christ and the eternal realm, we come to know Him more deeply and more appreciatively.

In many ways, it is easy to see how all things bear witness of the Creator. His creations are the perfect evidence of His presence. But as we look more deeply at the messages conveyed by the Creator within His creations, we learn much that escapes the casual observer. Many of those physical creations were chosen by the Creator Himself as to convey great spiritual truths. We can all see the outward or the physical presence, but the Creator has undoubtedly placed deeper spiritual meanings within many of His creations as well.

For example, olives are prominent throughout gospel teachings and were a common feature in the Savior's life because of the geographic area He lived in. He taught the essence of Christianity on the Mount of Olives. His Atonement was partly accomplished in a place whose name means "oil press," which is understood as referring to olive oil. Olive oil is also used throughout the scriptures to heal the sick and to set apart kings, priests, and prophets.

Why olives? Well, that's one of many wonderful subjects to ponder and explore in this book. The short answer is that their oil represents the Holy Ghost and was a principle source of light in biblical times.

Symbolism Is Essential to Full Gospel Understanding

Quite simply, there are many vital eternal lessons that we will never learn without an understanding of gospel symbolism. Specifically, the Lord's most precious lessons taught in the temple will pass through us like water through a sieve if we do not learn to think symbolically. We will have neither an understanding nor an appreciation of these most beautiful and eternal lessons if we don't gain a working understanding of gospel symbolism.

Throughout much of this earth's history, symbolism has been a necessary medium for teaching the Lord's children simply because printed scriptures have not been as readily available as they are now. Even when printed text was readily available, relatively few people were physically able to read. So, while reading printed words has been a part of our everyday lives for generations, earlier generations had to rely more on symbolism because of the sheer lack of written communication in their societies.

Likewise, there are almost certainly lessons in our own lives that the Lord has tried to teach us, or is trying now to teach us, that we will only learn with an understanding of symbolism. Nephi's admonition to "liken all scriptures unto us, that it might be for our profit and learning" (1 Nephi 19:23) is at least in part a lesson on symbolism.

How is the process of "likening the scriptures" an application of symbolism? The trials and triumphs in the scriptures are types and shadows (in other words, symbols) of our own trials and triumphs. For example, when we read of Adam and Eve's experiences in the garden of Eden; Abraham's actions; the Savior's temptations, miracles, and anguish; or Joseph Smith's pleadings in the Liberty Jail, we are meant to liken them unto ourselves—to put ourselves in their shoes—that it might be for our profit and learning. With this kind of symbolism, we don't just learn from scriptural experiences; we recognize those experiences as types and shadows of our own experiences in mortality.

When we long for the blessing of posterity, do we see ourselves as Abraham and Sarah? When we feel that we've earned the blessing we've worked so hard for, do we recognize the worth of another seven or so years of work to obtain it, like Jacob and Rachel? When we seem to lose the very blessing we have been praying for, do we recognize that we are climbing our own Mount Moriah, like Abraham and Isaac? Like the Israelites who had just been freed from captivity, do we recognize our own molten calf that we prize more than the words of the Lord that come through our own latter-day Moses?

Just as the Lord uses physical objects to convey spiritual truths, He also uses the experiences of His prophets to convey spiritual truths to us as we pass through our own wilderness like Lehi's family, our own Liberty Jail like Joseph Smith, or our own Egypt like Israel.

So you see, an understanding of gospel symbolism is really not intended just for the intellectual or the curious. Recognizing the hand of God in our own triumphs and trials deep in the refiner's fire is a truly personal lesson in gospel symbolism. The Lord wants each of us to learn the universal language of gospel symbolism so that we will understand the scriptures, the temple, and countless other lessons He may teach us throughout our lives.

Finding and Exploring Gold Mines

As we can already see, symbolism in the scriptures is too often overlooked. This may be by design, as symbolism has the unique ability both to reward the humble seeker of truth and to keep great lessons from the spiritually unprepared. Two people with different levels of spiritual understanding can look at a symbol and see two completely different things. The spiritually unprepared person will see only a hole in the ground, where the spiritually mature person will see a gold mine. Our challenge is not just to see the gold mine; it is to know how and where to look for the gold mine, and then to explore the mine.

There are a number of books written on gospel symbolism. For most of these books, the major message is what certain symbols found throughout the gospel mean. For example, a book like this may teach that olive oil represents the Holy Ghost, as we just learned. This kind of interpretative message should be in every symbolism book, and some books do a wonderful job of simply conveying those interpretations. Such books may be thought of as a guide to finding the gold mines we mentioned earlier.

In contrast, this book may be thought of as a guide to exploring those gold mines. The central message of this book is not just what certain symbols mean; it is why and how those symbols carry their particular meaning. When we understand, for example, how trees teach us about the Atonement and other gospel principles or why the earth's history and placement teaches about Christ, our appreciation for the Savior deepens. We find more and more treasures as we discover and explore the gold mines of gospel symbolism.

This gold mine exploration begins with the first of the Lord's creations: Earth itself. In the first section of this book we will explore how, on a broad scale, the earth's existence and history are lessons about the Savior. The Creation narrative also lists specific essentials that are both evidence and representations of the Creator. Light, water, rocks, and trees were all part of the Creation, and they all carry poignant lessons about their Creator. In the second section, we will see how the law given by the Lord and the prophets called by the Lord do more than lead us in the way of the Savior. They typify the Savior and help us understand Him with more depth and appreciation. Finally, in the third section of the book, we will discuss prominent scriptural symbols like salt, blood, and olives. These symbols are key parts of our life on earth, and they also contain great symbolic lessons about the Savior and His gospel.

I hope you will enjoy and learn from the discussions presented in this book.

NOTES

1. John A. Widtsoe, "Temple Worship," *Utah Genealogical and Historical Magazine* 12 (April 1921): 54.
2. Joseph Fielding Smith, Conference Report, October, 1958, 22.
3. David B. Haight, "The Sacrament—and the Sacrifice," *Ensign*, Nov. 1989, 59.
4. Ibid.
5. Herman Bangerter, as found in *Temples of the Most High*, comp. N. B. Lundwall (Salt Lake City: Bookcraft, 1952), 258.

SECTION ONE

Symbols in the Creation

Earth

Our mortal home actually teaches us many lessons about the plan of salvation. The prophet Brigham Young described Mother Earth as a living example of obedience for us to follow. "The earth is very good in and of itself and has abided a celestial law, consequently we should not despise it nor desire to leave it, but rather desire and strive to obey the same law that the earth abides and abide it as honorably as does the earth."[1] In this sense, as Nephi reminds us, it is even an example to us. "For behold, the dust of the earth moveth hither and thither, to the dividing asunder, at the command of our great and everlasting God" (Helaman 12:8).

As we look back on the Creation of this earth, we might first consider the time the Lord takes to teach us of this. According to the accounts recorded in Genesis, Moses, and Abraham, each stage of the Creation built upon the former. The matter was organized, the land was separated from the water, the greater and lesser lights were divided, all manner of plant life was created, animals were created, and finally man was created.

Notice that each stage of creation builds toward the grandest of all of God's creations: man. Land was given for man to live on. Water gave beauty and life to man's new home and provided him with a compound essential to his existence. Light was given to sustain his life. Plants were created not only for man's food, clothing, and shelter but to beautify his environment. Animals were given for man's sustenance and placed under his dominion.

Adam and Eve were sent forth from the Garden of Eden to till the earth and live from its fruits. When the two of them were driven out of the Garden of Eden, Adam was told that he would one day return to dust (see Genesis 3:19). This is a fate we all share. As sons and daughters of Adam and Eve, we pass through mortality, we die, and our spiritless bodies are laid to rest in the earth. In the resurrection, we will all spring forth to new and everlasting life, once again rising from the earth where our bodies have been laid to rest.

Following this pattern of Adam and Eve, the earth signifies the beginning of mortality, the substance of physical survival in mortality, the end of mortality, and the beginning of the resurrection and immortality. Throughout all of this, the earth is an example of obedience to us.

The Earth's History

We can see even more clearly the importance of the earth from a literary device known as a chiasmus that is used frequently in the scriptures. The chiasmus gains its name from the Greek letter chi (X), which closely resembles our "X." In an "X" we see two triangles, one on top and one on bottom, pointing toward a middle point where they meet. This middle point is the important concept that we are supposed to learn. The "ends" of the chiasmus point to and emphasize this middle point. Whenever we find a chiasmus pattern in the scriptures, the middle of it is the focal point and true lesson.

As it turns out, the earth is at the center of many chiastic patterns that emphasize the importance of mortality and the Savior's mission.

The Plan of Salvation

Our life is without beginning or end, and it is difficult to define eternity with our finite minds, but we can basically divide eternity into two parts: premortal and postmortal. These two parts are separated by the pinprick of time we spend here upon the earth in mortality. In this sense, both "ends" of eternity point to mortal life. As a chiasmus, it would look like this:

PREMORTAL LIFE
    MORTAL LIFE (EARTH LIFE)
POSTMORTAL LIFE

What is the Lord trying to teach us with this pattern? Amulek teaches us that all of eternity depends on what we do in this dot of time we spend on the earth. It is the center and pivotal point of our eternity.

> For behold, this life is the time for men to prepare to meet God; yea, behold the day of this life is the day for men to perform their labors.
>
> And now, as I said unto you before, as ye have had so many witnesses, therefore, I beseech of you that ye do not procrastinate the day of your repentance until the end; for after this day of life, which is given us to prepare for eternity, behold, if we do not improve our time while in this life, then cometh the night of darkness wherein there can be no labor performed.
>
> Ye cannot say, when ye are brought to that awful crisis, that I will repent, that I will return to my God. Nay, ye cannot say this; for that same spirit which doth possess your bodies at the time that ye go out of this life, that same spirit will have power to possess your body in that eternal world. (Alma 34:32–34)

Our very eternal state depends on what we do in this life. It is staggering to realize that eternity hinges on the blink of an eye that we call mortality. But that lesson is clear from the scriptures, and it is emphasized as the center point of the chiasmus that is the plan of salvation.

The Earth's Temporal History

Not only does the chiasmus of eternity emphasize the importance of mortality, but the history of the earth itself also emphasizes the importance of the very day in which we now live. When the earth was created, it was created spiritually and dwelt with God, a position to which it will return. The earth was then in a celestial state. Next, with the creation of Adam (before the Fall), man inhabited the earth. The earth enjoyed the partial but not full presence of the Father. The earth was then in a terrestrial state. After the Fall, the earth became, as it is now: a telestial dwelling. With the Millennium, the earth will be renewed to a terrestrial state. And then, finally, the earth will receive the celestial glory it had before.[2] For these stages, the word most commonly used is "renewed," as stated in the Thirteenth Article of Faith. This "renewal" implies that the earth will be restored to a former state.

As a chiasmus, it looks like this:

CELESTIAL STATE
  TERRESTRIAL STATE
    TELESTIAL STATE (how it is right now)
  TERRESTRIAL STATE
CELESTIAL STATE

Again, our current state is the focal point of the chiasmus. The lesson is that in order to return to a celestial state (or to return to the presence of our Heavenly Father), we must take advantage of the days of probation the Lord has given us in mortality. The central point around which celestial life revolves is this time of probation we spend on the earth.

The Earth's History Pointing to Christ

We are told that the earth has a temporal existence of seven thousand years (see D&C 77:7). Many prophecies of Christ refer to His coming in the "meridian [mid-point] of time" (Moses 5:57; 6:57, 62; 7:46). This time represents the true "high noon" of the earth's history. Not only is it a mid-point, it is the pinnacle. "The meridian of time is the middle or high point of that portion of eternity which is considered to be mortal time. Since Christ lived, ministered, and worked out the Atonement in time's meridian, such era was truly the high point of history."[3]

As a chiasmus, the very temporal existence of the earth points to and centers around Christ and His mortal ministry. Christ came at the end of the fourth millennium, or the meridian of time. Elder James E. Talmage dated the birth of the Savior at April 6, 1 BC.[4] Presidents Harold B. Lee[5] and Spencer W. Kimball[6] have made similar statements. Christ's first advent is significantly placed in the fourth of seven millennia. Four is often the number representing perfection in mortality (four corners of the earth, four seasons, and so on). Christ came in the meridian of time to bring perfection to the earth and to all of her inhabitants who would follow Him.

The first and seventh millennia also mark the presence of God with man on earth. The first millennium began with the Fall. Immediately before this, Adam and Eve enjoyed the personal presence of God in the Garden of Eden. The final millennium will be marked by the Second Coming.

FIRST THOUSAND YEARS
SECOND THOUSAND YEARS
THIRD THOUSAND YEARS
FOURTH THOUSAND YEARS
FIFTH THOUSAND YEARS
SIXTH THOUSAND YEARS
SEVENTH THOUSAND YEARS

As eternity centers around the time of our probation on the earth, this time on the earth centers on Christ. He is the focal point, the key to eternity. The presence of God marks the beginning, central point, and ending point of the earth's physical history. As the center point, Christ is the key to man's regaining the eternal presence of God.

The Earth's History and the Bible

The Bible—not just its teachings but the Bible itself—reinforces this same teaching. The word "testament" (as in Old and New Testament, the two parts of our Bible) is identical to the word "covenant" in the Greek language (*diatheke*).[7] One of Christ's many titles is "Mediator of the New Covenant" (D&C 76:69). He is the one to whom the covenants (the Old and New Testaments) point. He is the one who brings the testaments and covenants together:

OLD TESTAMENT (COVENANT)
ADVENT OF CHRIST
NEW TESTAMENT (COVENANT)

The coming of our Lord divides the Old and New Testament as it divides time as we measure it (BC—before Christ, and AD—anno domini or "the year of our Lord"). Both testaments testify of and point to Christ.

Summary

The earth itself—its placement and its history—points to Christ. In so doing, the earth teaches us who should be the center of our lives and who is constantly inviting us to come unto Him. The earth is our home and, through the Atonement of Christ, it is also our bridge back to the presence of God.

Notes

1. *Discourses of Brigham Young*, comp. John A. Widtsoe (Salt Lake City: The Deseret News Press, 1954), 101.
2. Bruce R. McConkie, *A New Witness for the Articles of Faith*, (Salt Lake City: Deseret Book, 1985), 648–50.
3. Bruce R. Mcconkie, *Mormon Doctrine* (Salt Lake City: Bookcraft, 1966), 486.
4. James E. Talmage, *Jesus the Christ* (Salt Lake City: Deseret Book, 1974), 104.
5. Harold B. Lee, Conference Report, May 1973.
6. Spencer W. Kimball, "Remarks and Dedication of the Fayette, New York, Buildings," *Ensign*, May 1980, 54.
7. James Strong, *Strong's Exhaustive Concordance of the Bible, with words of Jesus in red letter and key-word comparison of selected words and phrases in the King James Version with five leading translations*, (Iowa Falls: World Bible Publishers, 1986), Greek word 1242.

LIGHT

Within the Creation of the earth itself, we see the essentials to life on earth. The Creation accounts found in Genesis, Moses, and Abraham base the Creation around essential principles and substances that are indispensable to life on earth. Not surprisingly, each of these essential ingredients is a type of its creator. The Creation accounts begin with light. "And God said, Let there be light: and there was light. And God saw the light, that it was good: and God divided the light from the darkness" (Genesis 1:3–4).

LIGHT AND THE CREATION

Why does the Creation begin with light? Light represents Jesus Christ, as He is the Light of the World (see John 8:12; 9:5; Mosiah 16:9; Alma 38:9; 3 Nephi 9:18; 11:11; 18:16; D&C 10:70). In the Americas, the earthly arrival of the Light of the World was marked by a day, a night, and a day with no darkness (see Helaman 14:4; 3 Nephi 1:8, 15). Likewise, when the Light of the World was taken, darkness covered the earth for the space of three days (see 3 Nephi 8:20–23). In these cases, the physical light and darkness were a representation of the Light of the World coming into and then departing from the world.

As Elder Bruce R. McConkie taught,

> Gospel light is the mental and spiritual enlightenment from God which enables men to receive truth and knowledge and gain salvation.

> Light is an attribute of Deity and shines forth from him; in it is found its fulness and perfection. ". . . God is light, and in him is no darkness at all" (1 John 1:5); he is "the Father of lights." (James 1:17).
>
> Christ is the light of the world, and the gospel is his message of light and salvation to all men. "I have sent mine everlasting covenant into the world," he said, speaking of the restoration of the gospel, "to be a light to the world, and to be a standard for my people, and for the Gentiles to seek to it." (D&C 45:9)[1]

Christ is more than just the source of gospel light. According to John Taylor (and not surprising given the light and darkness that accompanied the Savior's birth and crucifixion), Christ is also the source of literal light. "God is light and in him there is no darkness. He is the light of the sun and the power thereof by which it was made; he is also the light of the moon and the power by which it was made; he is the light of the stars and the power by which they were made. He says it [light] is the same light that enlightens the understanding of men. What, have we a mental light and a visual light, all proceeding from the same source? Yes, so says the scripture, and so says science when rightly comprehended."[2]

All light, like its Source, has the same purpose: to illuminate, lead, and give life. Parley P. Pratt explained:

> This is the true light, which in some measure illuminates all men. It is, in its less refined particles, the physical light which reflects from the sun, moon and stars, and other substances; and by reflection on the eye, makes visible the truths of the outward world.
>
> It is, also, in its higher degrees, the intellectual light of our inward and spiritual organs, by which we reason, discern, judge, compare, comprehend and remember the subjects within our reach.
>
> Its inspiration constitutes instinct in animal life, reason in man, vision in the Prophets, and is continually flowing from the Godhead throughout all His creatures.[3]

There is no life without light. There is no vision without light. No life-sustaining plants can grow without light. Quite simply, there is no life in the world without the Light of the World.

Our Source of Light: The Sun

The center of our solar system and the physical source of our light, life, and preservation here on earth is the sun. In English the words "sun" and "son" are nearly identical in form, even though they mean very different things. Malachi 4:2 prophesies of the Second Coming by foretelling the "Sun of righteousness" arising with "healing in his wings." The Book of Mormon rendition of this scripture in 3 Nephi 25:2 changes the spelling to "Son," but the spelling in Malachi may not be a complete mistake or a coincidence. The parallels between the Sun and the Son suggest that at least in this case the two nouns are closely related in their purpose and effect. The sun teaches lessons about the Son of God.

Consider the parallels:

- The sun is the center of our solar system. It provides all of the substantial light for the planets within its system. The earth is opaque and does not emit light by itself; therefore, we depend on the sun for all of our light.
- The sun surpasses all other globes in the system in both magnitude and splendor. In the same manner, the Son of God surpasses all in intelligence (see Abraham 3:19).
- The sun shines on all of the earth, just as the Light of Christ shines on every man (see John 1:9). In fact, this source of light appears inexhaustible to mankind. If mankind could fully harness all the light from the sun that falls on earth, it would be an endless supply of energy.
- The light of the sun cannot touch anything on earth without bringing about a change in it, whether chemical or mechanical. Receiving the light of the Savior likewise brings a mighty change of heart (see Alma 5:14).

There would be no life on earth without the sun. It is the source of all the light and warmth on earth. Without it, there would be no warmth and no growth. Even the most barren of arctic wastelands receives a fair degree of light and warmth from the sun. By contrast, this same wasteland is a Garden of Eden compared to a land without any sunlight. By the same token, there is no life without the Son of God, the light and life of the world (see 3 Nephi 11:11).[4]

A great many of the most poignant observations about our sun are lessons about the Son of God.

What We Do with Light

The light of the sun fills the immensity of space, but life, especially human life, is only found in a small part of the solar system. The vast solar system receives the same light from the sun that we do on earth, yet that light alone doesn't foster life as it does on earth.

Why? In physical terms, light must be both reflected and absorbed to create conditions where life can thrive. Through its reflection and absorption of light (and through the presence of oxygen), the earth's atmosphere presents an environment that provides a home for the greatest of God's creations: man. The expanse of space, for the most part, does not have an atmosphere to capture, reflect, and absorb the sun's light. So that expanse remains too cold and empty to support life.

In spiritual terms, our level of life depends on how well we reflect and absorb the light of the Son. We reflect His light by being spiritually born of Him (see Alma 5:14) and by sharing His light with others (see Matthew 5:14–16). Spiritually speaking, we also absorb His light by living by every word that He gives us (see Matthew 4:4). A light as powerful as His can't help but shine to others (see Matthew 5:14–16). Through reflecting and absorbing the Light of the World, we enjoy an increased level of spiritual life for ourselves and we perpetuate that life for others.

Too Much Sun

At the same time, too much sun can destroy. Like many symbolic representations of the Lord, the sun must be kept within certain bounds to be a blessing and not a curse. When we do not follow the bounds of wisdom and balance with the sun, we can be scorched, burned, and even destroyed. As with the other symbols of Christ that will be discussed, the sun can represent something helpful—if it is applied within the bounds the Lord has set—or it can represent something woeful—if it is applied outside of those bounds.

In the case of light, one beneficial way to view its potential symbolic meanings is by thinking of the bounds of priesthood and worthiness. Just as the priesthood is a protection that allows us to see the face of God and live (see D&C 84:22), we cannot tolerate the full presence of the sun without a shield. A shield from the physical sun may be a roof, an umbrella, proper clothing, a tree, or a cloud. Our shield from the spiritual effects of the Son of God is the protective covering of the priesthood and the priesthood ordinances that are only received by those who are worthy.

GRAVITY

The sun also serves as the gravitational center of the solar system. The earth is kept constant in its orbit by the gravitational pull of the sun. Gravity is a particularly peculiar phenomenon. It exists between any two objects anywhere. It is an attraction that pulls those two objects together. Our finite minds might consider light to be the fastest thing in our realm, but if anything temporal is instantaneous, it may well be gravity. It is present everywhere and, as far as we can tell, is not subject to time.

I have blamed countless accidents on gravity throughout my life, but the truth is that gravity holds the very universe together, much like the Spirit that emanates from Christ. Without gravity, everything would either float around completely without order or do something so extraordinary that our minds would not even be able to picture it. We simply don't know what would happen in the universe without gravity because gravity is omnipresent.

The strength of a gravitational attraction depends on two things: an object's mass (which is a measure of inertia, or resistance to change in speed or motion) and the proximity between objects. The gravitational attraction between two objects can therefore be increased either by increasing the mass of the objects or by bringing the two objects closer together. There is a symbolic lesson in this law of gravity.

We are promised that the Lord will draw near unto us if we will draw near unto Him (see D&C 88:63). Symbolically speaking, the gravitational attraction between us and the Lord will increase dramatically as our movement toward Him is rewarded with His reciprocal movement toward us. And just as the sun keeps the earth in motion, He is already sustaining us, whether we realize it or not (see Mosiah 2:21).

In our solar system, the sun is by far the most massive body. Its position within the system does not change, as all the planets rotate around it. The prophet Nephi understood this principle of eternal constants and the center of the solar system centuries before Galileo (see Helaman 12:15). The Son of God likewise is the greatest of all children of God and is the same yesterday, today, and always (see Hebrews 13:8). He is the eternal constant. His grandeur is so incomprehensible that all are invited to come unto Him, and no one is excluded from the invitation (see 2 Nephi 26: 25, 27, 33). There is room for everyone at the Savior's table, and that table is always open.

The laws of gravity typify the relationship we have and are invited to have with the Son of God. The closer planets come in their orbit around the sun, the more light and warmth they receive, and the more rapidly they travel in their orbit. By the same token, the closer we come to Him, the thinner the veil becomes, the more light and truth we receive, and the more rapidly we progress. In this sense, the natural law of gravity is a perfect illustration of a spiritual law.

The Sun, the Moon, and the Stars

Paul's famous scripture describing the kingdoms of glory and the resurrection compares those kingdoms to the Sun, the moon, and the stars. "There are also celestial bodies, and bodies terrestrial: but the glory of the celestial is one, and the glory of the terrestrial is another. There is one glory of the sun, and another glory of the moon, and another glory of the stars: for one star differeth from another star in glory. So also is the resurrection of the dead" (1 Corinthians 15:40–42). Section 76 of the Doctrine and Covenants teaches more on the subject by describing the qualifications and characteristics of those who inherit each kingdom (see D&C 76:70–71, 78, 81, 96–98).

The important lesson in Paul's analogy is that our resurrection and eternity are based on the levels of light that we receive and embrace. Those who make and keep the highest covenants inherit the greatest light in the celestial kingdom (see D&C 76:50–70). Those who make and keep lesser covenants inherit a lesser light (see D&C 76:71–106).

Of all the descriptions of eternity that could have been used, the Lord has chosen to measure and explain the resurrection and kingdoms of glory in terms of light. Our testimony of the Savior and our application of His Atonement determine the level of light and the eternal reward that we receive.

Light and Revelation

To reveal (as in "revelation") literally means to draw back the veil.

Throughout scriptural history, the Lord has used instruments whose names refer to lights to bring about revelation and draw back the veil. "Urim and Thummim" means "lights and perfections" in Hebrew.[5] As Christ is the source of light (see D&C 93:9), drawing nearer to Him draws back the veil and brings us more light. This truth is embodied in the first part of this term, urim, which means "lights." Christ is also the Perfect One. As we approach Him, we come closer to perfection. This is the truth embodied in the second part of the term, thummim, which means "perfections."

Light and perfection are the keys to help us rend the veil. The Doctrine and Covenants illustrates this perfectly. "Verily, thus saith the Lord: It shall come to pass that every soul who forsaketh his sins and cometh unto me, and calleth on my name, and obeyeth my voice, and keepeth my commandments, shall see my face and know that I am; And that I am the true light that lighteth every man that cometh into the world" (D&C 93:1–2).

Drawing back the veil automatically leads to receiving more light, even the spirit of prophecy and the testimony of Jesus (see Revelation 19:10). Throughout the history of revelation on the earth, the Lord has often given such light and revelation through a Urim and Thummim. John A. Widtsoe explained,

> The sacred instrument known as the Urim and Thummim, "two stones in silver bows," accompanied the Book of Mormon plates and was used by Joseph Smith in the translation of the Book of Mormon. For some time it was used also in securing revelations from the Lord. The use of this instrument is an evidence of the truth of the Prophet's story of his spiritual experiences leading to the work entrusted to him.
>
> The Urim and Thummim is mentioned in the Bible in connection with priestly functions. It was to be used in making the will of the Lord clear and comprehensible to the priest. Aaron was instructed to wear the Urim and Thummim "upon the heart," when he went to secure "judgment" from the Lord; and his successors were instructed to use the Urim and Thummim when they asked "counsel" from the Lord. Clearly, the Urim and Thummim was used in early days in official communications with the Lord. Beyond that, little is known of it.
>
> The use of physical aids to help man in sacred work is age-old. Enoch, Noah, Abraham, Moses, Aaron, and the later prophets used such means in their work.

Such helps are mentioned also in the Book of Mormon. Mosiah speaks of the possession of the Urim and Thummim by the Jaredites. The brother of Jared molded sixteen small stones, which after being touched by God, became luminous and gave light on the voyage across the ocean. Lehi on the way to the ocean found the Liahona which was used to guide them in traveling over the ocean.

Such helps were not confined to translation as in the case of Joseph Smith, but also for giving light and setting the course of travel.

How such aids to human senses operate is not known. Divine power, using the forces of the universe, set them in motion for those who are authorized to employ them in their work. It seems probable that they demand an intense concentration upon the theme in mind, which brings about the communion with divine forces, necessary to do the required work, such as translation of unknown languages. The instrument itself is valueless unless used by an authorized person.[6]

Summary

There would be no life without light. Just as the sun is the source of all natural light in our mortal realm, the Son of God is the source of all gospel light in the spiritual realm. His light fills the immensity of all space (see D&C 88:12). It is His light that is in all things and that gives life to all things (see D&C 88:13). He is the source of all gospel light and the one who allows us to draw back the veil.

Notes

1. McConkie, *Mormon Doctrine*, 444.
2. John Taylor, *Journal of Discourses*, 18:330; accessed via GospeLink.com.
3. Parley P. Pratt, *Key to the Science of Theology*, (Salt Lake City: Deseret Book, 1855), 41; accessed via GospeLink.com.
4. The observations in this section come from Herbert W. Morris, *The Celestial Symbol Interpreted* (Philadelphia: J. C. McCurdy & Co., 1883).
5. Strong, *Strong's Exhaustive Concordance of the Bible,* Hebrew words 224 and 8550.
6. John A. Widtsoe, *Joseph Smith–Seeker after Truth, Prophet of God* (Salt Lake City: Bookcraft, 1950), 265–66; accessed via GospeLink.com.

Water

Moving from the earth as a whole to other creations on the earth, we find more types of Christ and more physical phenomena that represent spiritual laws and principles. One of the most prominent components of the earth itself is water. Like light, water is essential to our existence.

As with the earth and light, water symbolically points to Christ. "Living water is the words of eternal life, the message of salvation, the truths about God and his kingdom; it is the doctrines of the gospel."[1] Quite simply Christ is the fountain of living waters (see Jeremiah 2:13). Life, cleanliness, refreshment, and all of the other blessings that come from water are symbolically associated with the living water flowing from Him.

Water as a Cleanser

Water is known for its cleansing power. Brigham Young taught,

> Pure water is cleansing—it serves to purify; and you are aware the ancient Saints were very tenacious with regard to their purification by water. From the beginning the Lord instituted water for that purpose among others. I do not mean from the beginning of this earth alone; and although we have not immediate concern in inquiring into the organization of other earths that do not come within reach of our investigation, yet I will say that water has been the means of purification in every world that has been organized out of the immensity of matter.[2]

We cannot imagine washing ourselves, our clothes, or our homes without water. Spiritually speaking, we also rely on water to wash us of our sins. "But, behold, the days of thy deliverance are come, if thou wilt hearken to my voice, which saith unto thee: Arise and be baptized, and wash away your sins, calling on my name, and you shall receive my Spirit, and a blessing so great as you never have known" (D&C 39:10). The ordinance of baptism washes us of sin and allows us to enter into the Savior's Church on earth and receive the greater blessings of the Lord's Spirit.

Paul also spoke of water as an agent for cleansing in a different way. "Husbands, love your wives, even as Christ also loved the church, and gave himself for it; That he might sanctify and cleanse it with the washing of water by the word" (Ephesians 5:25–26).

Anciently, Aaron and his sons used water to wash themselves before they entered into the tabernacle (see Exodus 29:4). This washing ordinance is also part of the temple experience in the restored gospel (see D&C 124:37–39). In both the ancient and latter-day churches, washing with water allows members of the Church to enter the Lord's house. This paves the way for still greater blessings promised to the faithful in the house of the Lord (see D&C 124:39–41).

With both the ordinances of baptism and the temple, the blessing of being washed clean with water opens the doors to even greater blessings. The washing accomplished by the water is only half a blessing. Spiritual cleanliness is its own reward, but it places us in a position to receive even more and greater blessings from the Lord in His Church and then again in His house, the temple.

Water as a Source of Life

The Creation accounts actually begin with water as the source of life. The "Spirit of God moved upon the face of the waters" to begin the Creation of the earth (Genesis 1:2). In this sense, water is the starting point for life on earth. Like the "birth" of our earthly home, our own physical birth—in both a physical and spiritual sense—comes through water.

> By reason of transgression cometh the fall, which fall bringeth death, and inasmuch as ye were born into the world by water, and blood, and the spirit, which I have made, and so became of dust a living soul, even so ye must be born again into the kingdom of heaven, of water, and of the Spirit, and be cleansed by blood, even the blood of

> mine Only Begotten; that ye might be sanctified from all sin, and enjoy the words of eternal life in this world and eternal life in the world to come, even immortal glory. (Moses 6:59)

True to the theme of gospel symbolism, the emblem of water in our physical birth points to water as an emblem of our spiritual rebirth.

> There was a man of the Pharisees, named Nicodemus, a ruler of the Jews:
>
> The same came to Jesus by night, and said unto him, Rabbi, we know that thou art a teacher come from God: for no man can do these miracles that thou doest, except God be with him.
>
> Jesus answered and said unto him, Verily, verily, I say unto thee, Except a man be born again, he cannot see the kingdom of God.
>
> Nicodemus saith unto him, How can a man be born when he is old? can he enter the second time into his mother's womb, and be born?
>
> Jesus answered, Verily, verily, I say unto thee, Except a man be born of water and of the Spirit, he cannot enter into the kingdom of God.
>
> That which is born of the flesh is flesh; and that which is born of the Spirit is spirit.
>
> Marvel not that I said unto thee, Ye must be born again. (John 3:1–7)

Water not only gives physical and spiritual life, it sustains that life. The human body can survive for weeks without food, but only a few days without water. Plant and animal life expires shortly without water. This symbolically illustrates our constant need for the Lord. "Jesus answered and said unto [the woman of Samaria], If thou knewest the gift of God, and who it is that saith to thee, Give me to drink; thou wouldest have asked of him, and he would have given thee living water . . . whosoever drinketh of the water that I shall give him shall never thirst; but the water that I shall give him shall be in him a well of water springing up into everlasting life" (John 4:10, 14).

In the vision given to Lehi and later to his son Nephi, we see even more of the significance of Christ as the fountain of living waters. "And it came to pass that I beheld that the rod of iron, which my father had seen, was the word of God, which led to the fountain of living waters, or to the tree of life; which waters are a representation of the love of God; and I also beheld that the tree of life was a representation of the love of God" (1 Nephi 11:25).

Water or "living water" symbolizes the love of God. The love of God is manifest and personified in Christ. Because of this, our spiritual birth and continued spiritual life are wholly dependent on Christ. Just as water flows from its fountain, life and blessings flow from Christ.

Water is given as a token of the love of God (see 1 Nephi 11:25). Smith's Bible Dictionary also proclaims water as an emblem of spiritual blessings or salvation.[3] Especially with these symbols, it is important to remember the source of water. That source is Christ (see John 4; Jeremiah 2:13; 17:13).

The Earth's Hydrologic System

Water can be even better understood as a gospel symbol when we examine the hydrologic system, or the system by which water is circulated around the earth. About 97.5 percent of the world's water is contained in the seas.[4] These are saltwater bodies. In fact, the Greek word for sea, *thalassa* is derived from *hals*, which means salt.[5]

In the hydrologic system, water is collected in and evaporates from the seas. From there it circulates with the atmosphere and is eventually precipitated as rain or snow on the land. Most of the water that falls on the land returns to the seas by surface runoff and groundwater seepage.

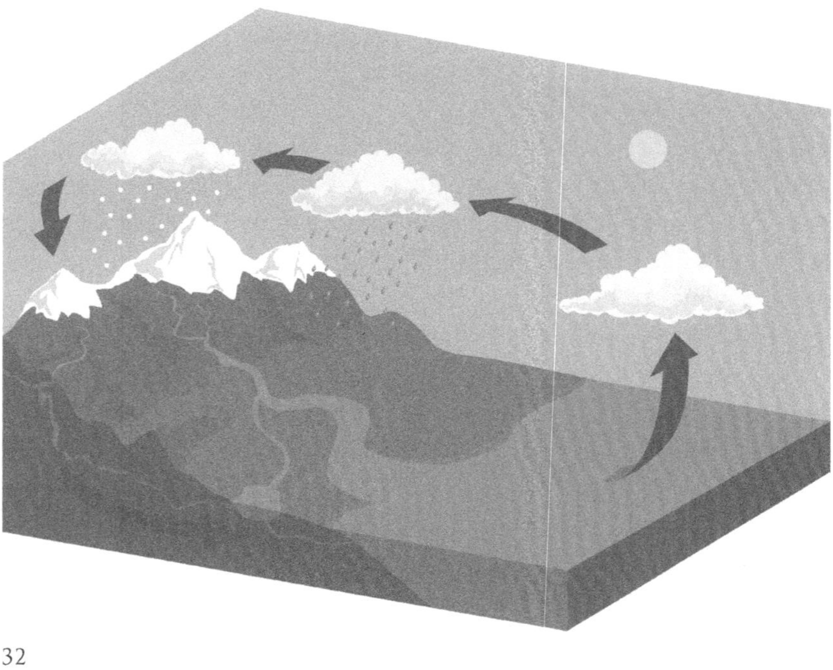

WHAT SYMBOLISM DOES THIS MODEL CARRY?

The sea is the vast collection point of water (symbolic of the message of salvation). In the sea, that collected water is mixed with salt. From there, the water evaporates because of the same force that drives the entire system: warmth and heat from the sun. (For our purposes we could spell it "Son.") The water is then carried to the land or the world (i.e., us) by wind.[6]

The word for "wind" in Hebrew is *ruwach*, which is identical to the word for "spirit."[7] In other words, it is the Spirit that brings the water (gospel truths, blessings, and so on) to the land, or people. From there the water falls to the earth as rain, which is also a symbol for blessings from on high (see Leviticus 26:3–4). The rain is drawn to the earth by gravity just as the earth is drawn to the sun (Son) and kept in its orbit by gravity. This water brings life to the earth and everything on it. Finally the rivers return their water to the sea, their gathering place separated from the land.

In Church leadership meetings I have attended, there is often talk of how to "get the water to the end of every row." This language comes from a farmer's perspective, expressing the need to get the blessings and message of the gospel to each member, even and especially those who are not easily reached. In a very real way, the answer of how to get the water to the end of the row is found in the earth's hydrologic system: It is done with the *ruwach*—the wind, the Spirit, the Holy Ghost. The Holy Ghost is the best and only way to convey the gospel message to all, especially those who seem difficult to reach.

Each part of the hydrologic process is indispensable. Without the sun (representing Christ), there would be no evaporation. The water would remain in the seas, never reaching the land or its inhabitants. Without the wind (representing the Holy Ghost), the water would evaporate but would fall right back into the ocean, as the clouds would never move. The land and all the life on it would remain parched and would soon become uninhabitable. Without gravity (another typification of Christ, as already noted), the water would evaporate and be circulated, but it would never reach the earth or flow back to the sea. Likewise each member of the Godhead is indispensable in the roles He plays in the plan of salvation. The lessons of the Savior abound, but perhaps we too easily forget or underappreciate the role of the Holy Ghost as the messenger of the Godhead.

Rivers, Water, and Cutting Covenants

Water is also a symbol of entering into a covenant. As Enoch explained, "by the water ye keep the commandment" (Moses 6:60). The symbolism in the concept of water representing covenants is remarkable when viewed in light of Old Testament covenant practices. It is the flow of water toward the sea that brings about stream erosion or stream cutting, the most common natural feature or landform on the earth. No matter where we are on the earth, within a few feet of us there is evidence of streams cutting downward toward the sea. These rivers—whether as great as the Mississippi or as tiny as condensation dripping down a window—are the most common method of transportation for water and the salt it collects from the earth.

The Hebrews used this phenomenon to teach lessons of steadfastness in keeping the Lord's commandments. Exhorting his wayward sons to follow the Lord, Lehi cried, "O that thou mightest be like unto this river, continually running into the fountain of all righteousness!" Likewise he pled, "O that thou mightest be like unto this valley, firm and steadfast, and immovable in keeping the commandments of the Lord!" (1 Nephi 2:9–10).

This is where covenant-making comes into play. The Hebrew word for covenant is *berith*, which implies cutting or passing between pieces of flesh.[8] This is what happened when the Abrahamic Covenant was made.[9] Smith's Bible Dictionary explains this relation between "cutting" and "covenant" as "sacrificing victims, dividing the parts, and both parties to the covenant walking between the parts of the sacrifice."[10] In our modern language, we "make" or "enter into" a covenant. In Hebrew, one "cut" a covenant.

This word *berith* comes from the root *barah*, which means to select, render clear, or choose.[11] In other words, it is through covenant that God's people are selected, chosen, and rendered clear from the rest of the world. As a "peculiar people," this is precisely what those who are set apart from the world do. Through baptism in the Lord's Church, they "cut" the waters and become a people uniquely "known" by the Lord out of "all the families of the earth" (Amos 3:2). This "cutting" follows the pattern of Moses' dividing or "cutting" the waters to escape from Egypt, which is a scriptural representation of the world.

Notice a recurring theme in the beginning of the Doctrine and Covenants: "Behold, I am God; give heed unto my word, which is quick and powerful, sharper than a two-edged sword, to the *dividing asunder* of both joints and marrow; therefore give heed unto my words" (D&C 6:2, emphasis added). This phrase appears in three other places in this same part of the Doctrine and Covenants (see D&C 11:2; 12:2; 14:2). The concept of "dividing asunder joints and marrow" illustrates the impact that covenants are intended to have on us. They are meant to penetrate us and form the core of who we really are. This is the same principle of inward devotion expressed by the prophet Jeremiah. "Behold the days come, saith the Lord, that I will make a new covenant with the house of Israel, and with the house of Judah . . . But this shall be the covenant that I will make with the house of Israel; After those days, saith the Lord, I will put my law in their inward parts, and write it in their hearts; and will be their God, and they shall be my people" (Jeremiah 31:31, 33). Covenant making or "cutting" is the Lord's process of writing His law inside of us, so to speak. It is the process by which He puts that law in our hearts, where our deepest and sincerest desires are.

Another purpose of covenants also fits with the theme of "cutting" covenants; essentially, the central purpose of covenants is to "cut" the veil between man and God and bring us back into the presence of our Heavenly Father. John teaches us that when Jesus completed His sacrifice, and thereby made it possible to remove the barrier between man and God, He said, "It is finished: and he bowed his head, and gave up the ghost" (John 19:30). The accounts in Matthew, Mark, and Luke go on to tell us that "the veil of the temple was rent in twain from the top to the bottom; and the earth did quake, and the rocks rent" (Matthew 27:51; Mark 15:38; Luke 23:45).

When the price of sin was paid, the veil was rent. The barrier between man and God had been overcome, torn right up the middle. Man was now enabled to return to his Heavenly Father if he would only take advantage of the Savior's veil-rending sacrifice. We can take advantage of that sacrifice and rend the veil through "cutting" or, in more familiar words, "making" or "entering into" covenants and then keeping those covenants.

"Covenant" is not the only word that has reference to cutting. The word "temple" comes from the Latin and Greek root *tem*, which also denotes cutting, or more specifically the "intersection of two lines at right angles."[12] The temple is the house of God and the place where the highest covenants are made. As we make these covenants, our will is joined with God's will.

The "intersection of two lines at right angles" forms the symbol of the square, an expression of precision. It also marks the intersecting of a vertical or divine force and a horizontal or terrestrial force. In other words, it is in the temple that we learn exactness and that our "cutting" or covenanting brings us as earthly beings in communion with Deity and the celestial realm. In the temple eternity meets our earthly realm and our will is brought into harmony with the will of God. If we are diligent and exact in keeping the covenants we make within the temple, we will one day be physically and literally brought into harmony of purpose with God; we will be brought into His presence. Again, the concepts of "cutting" and covenanting lead the way out of Egypt, or the world, and to a promised land of communion with God.

Rivers also marked the boundaries of the Garden of Eden, the first temple on earth.[13] Out of the Garden of Eden flowed four rivers, the Pison, Gihon, Euphrates, and Hiddekel (see Genesis 2:11–14). These rivers flowed out of the Garden to bless the land. In this case, the rivers carry two symbolic meanings. First, these rivers flowed from the first temple on the earth—the Garden of Eden. Like the waters that flowed from the temple in Ezekiel's vision (see Ezekiel 47), waters of healing also flowed from this temple. The rivers, therefore, teach us that the temple is the source of living water, or the blessings of the Lord.

Second, these rivers marked the boundaries of the temple. Crossing these rivers meant either exiting or re-entering the sanctuary of Eden. Joseph Smith spoke of our responsibility to "spread the light and truth of the everlasting Gospel from the rivers to the ends of the earth."[14] In other words, we have the responsibility to preach the gospel to every part of the world outside of the temple, to extend the boundaries of sacred ground to cover all the earth. The space within the rivers is sacred ground. The space outside of the rivers is what is often referred to as the "mission field." Crossing the rivers symbolizes entering into a covenant and entering or returning to sacred space. This is the same symbolic lesson taught when Joshua led the Israelites across the river Jordan to enter the promised land (see Joshua 4). In general, the act of crossing rivers symbolizes entering into a covenant and setting foot on sacred ground.

Summary

The fact that water is mentioned at the beginning of the Creation emphasizes its necessity for earth life. Just as water is essential to physical life, its symbolic meaning—the blessings of the gospel—are essential to spiritual life. In considering all of the physical and spiritual blessings of water, we must look to the fountain of living water: the Lord Jesus Christ.

NOTES

1. Bruce R. McConkie, *Doctrinal New Testament Commentary* (Salt Lake City: Bookcraft, 1990).
2. *Discourses of Brigham Young*, comp. John A. Widtsoe, 160.
3. *Smith's Bible Dictionary*, (Westwood, NJ: Barbour and Company, 1987), 64.
4. Kenneth W. Hamblin, *The Earth's Dynamic Systems* (Upper Saddle River, NJ: Prentice Hall), 23.
5. Strong, *Strong's Exhaustive Concordance of the Bible*, Greek word 2281.
6. Hamblin, *The Earth's Dynamic Systems*, 22.
7. Strong, *Strong's Exhaustive Concordance of the Bible,* Hebrew word 7307.
8. Ibid., Hebrew word 1285.
9. Genesis adds more information:

> And he said unto him, Take me an heifer of three years old, and a she goat of three years old, and a ram of three years old, and a turtle-dove, and a young pigeon.
>
> And he took unto him all these and *divided* them in the midst . . .
>
> And it came to pass, that, when the sun went down, and it was dark, behold a smoking furnace, and a burning lamp that passed between those pieces.
>
> In the same day the Lord made a covenant with Abram. (Genesis 15:9–10, 17–18, emphasis added)

10. *Smith's Bible Dictionary*, 64.
11. Strong, *Strong's Exhaustive Concordance of the Bible,* Hebrew word 1262.
12. Hugh Nibley, *Mormonism and Early Christianity*, (Salt Lake City: Deseret Book, 1987), 358.
13. Donald W. Parry, "Garden of Eden: Prototype Sanctuary," in *Temples of the Ancient World: Ritual and Symbolism*, ed. Donald W. Parry (Salt Lake City: Deseret Book, 1994), 126–51.
14. Joseph Smith, Jr., Diary 1835–1836, accessed via GospeLink.com; see also Joseph Smith, *History of the Church*, (Salt Lake City: Shadow Mountain, 1991), 2:375.

Rocks

Another significant part of the Creation was the separation of the dry land from the waters (see Genesis 1:9–10). This dry land consists mostly of rock.

The Book of Mormon refers to the Savior as "the rock" upon whom we must build our foundation (Helaman 5:12). Even before He was born into mortality, Moses and David called Him the Rock (see Deuteronomy 32:4; Psalms 28:1; 31:3; 42:9; 62:2; 78:35). To Enoch, the premortal Messiah referred to Himself as the "Rock of Heaven, which is broad as eternity" (Moses 7:53).

In latter-day revelation, His gospel is called a rock, as it is our only sure foundation (see D&C 11:24; 18:4–5; 33:12–13). Wise men will always choose this foundation to build on.

Christ, likewise, is the only solid foundation on which we can build. The first principle of the gospel is not simply faith but faith in Him. The Rock is a most fitting title for the Savior. No matter where you go on the earth, you will notice that there are two basic elements that are used to build shelters. One is wood, or some other tree product (stay tuned for more on this subject). The other is stone, or rock materials from the earth. Webster's defines "stone" as the material forming rock or as a rock itself, so we will use the two terms interchangeably.[1] Stone is solid, powerful, and referred to many times in the scriptures as the most sure foundation on which to build.

No matter where we go on the earth, rock supports and underlies us. Even the ocean is ultimately supported by rock. It would be difficult to imagine the earth without rock because the earth basically is rock with some other features such as water and dirt added.

All of these physical facts are also lessons that can point us to Christ. Christ is the one we have to thank for our lives here upon the earth. He is the Creator of the earth and all things on it (see Mosiah 3:8). It was by His light that this very earth was created (see D&C 88:7–10). No matter where we go on the earth, He is the one who supports us and preserves us.

In the Book of Mormon, there are two accounts of righteous people who were chosen of the Lord and told to flee from the rest of their people who were waxing into apostasy. The only place they could find safety and protection was in the cavity of a rock (see 1 Nephi 3:27; Ether 13:13–14, 22). As Christ is the Rock, we too have only one source of ultimate protection and eternal life.

The Sacrament and the Rock of Christ

It is plain to see that rocks are an apt symbol of our Redeemer.

> And now, my sons, remember, remember that it is upon the rock of our Redeemer, who is Christ, the Son of God, that ye must build your foundation; that when the devil shall send forth his mighty winds, yea, his shafts in the whirlwind, yea, when all his hail and his mighty storm shall beat upon you, it shall have no power over you to drag you down to the gulf of misery and endless wo, because of the rock upon which ye are built, which is a sure foundation, a foundation whereon if men build they cannot fall. (Helaman 5:12)

Aside from reiterating that Christ is the Rock, this scripture teaches of the blessings that come from being established upon His foundation. We can be protected from all of the adversary's woes if we are founded upon this Rock. How can we obtain this greatest of all defenses? Looking to 3 Nephi 18, where the Savior instituted the sacramental ordinance among the Nephites, we see the steps to becoming founded upon this Rock.

Bread

The chapter begins with Christ assembling those who would be His apostles and gathering the emblems of the sacrament. The first emblem of the sacrament is the bread. Jesus taught that He was the Bread of Life (see

John 6:35). Bethlehem, His birthplace, literally means "house of bread."[2] Additionally, manna was given to the children of Israel as they sojourned in the wilderness to represent the bread of life, who is Christ (see John 6:31–35).

Why did the Savior choose bread to represent Himself? Bread is a main staple throughout the world. Along with water, bread is the most basic food necessary for survival. In addition, "Bread, a common but important element of the diet during biblical times, played a crucial role in sustaining physical life. Perhaps it was for this reason that the Lord gave a sermon comparing himself to bread."[3]

Throughout the centuries, the chief ingredient of bread has been wheat. In the scriptures, wheat is given as a representation of the righteous or those to whom the Lord gives growth (see Matthew 13:36–43). Wheat flour is also traditionally ground by stone, which as we already know is another symbol of Christ. In bread, thousands of wheat kernels are gathered together, just as the saints are gathered together in the Church that belongs to the Bread of Life.[4]

The Lord taught both the Jews and the Nephites that the bread of the sacrament represented His body (see Matthew 26:26; 3 Nephi 18:7–11). As part of the sacrament ordinance, the bread is torn, just as Christ's body was torn on the cross. Partaking of the sacrament represents not only the Atonement but also our own membership in the Church. When Christ gave the bread to His disciples, they were given a time for reflection—exactly as the sacrament should be administered today. "And when they had eaten and were filled, he commanded that they should give unto the multitude" (3 Nephi 18:4). The disciples took the time to be "filled" in order to receive a fulness. When we eat, the nourishment we receive is distributed to every part of our bodies. That is what it means to be filled. When partaking of the sacrament, we should allow the nourishment—both physical and spiritual—to fill our entire bodies, our temples. We should be filled with the staple food of life and the staple is the Church or body of Christ. Partaking of the bread is the first step to becoming founded on the Rock of Christ.

The Rock as a Source of Water

Paul expounded on the comparison between bread and Christ's

body when he compared the veil in the temple to the body of Christ (see Hebrews 10:20). Paul uses the tearing of the Savior's body as a symbol for the veil in the temple, which is itself symbolic of the veil between man and God. When the Savior's flesh was torn, His precious atoning blood began to flow, just as it had the night before in Gethsemane. Paul taught that this tearing gave us "boldness to enter into the holiest by the blood of Jesus" (Hebrews 10:19). This is a reference to the veil of the temple that was rent or torn, just like the body of Christ, when the Savior had finished His mortal ministry (see Matthew 27:51; Mark 15:38; Luke 23:45). With this veil torn, man was symbolically and literally free to apply the blood of the Lamb and "enter into the holiest," or the presence of God.

This leads us to the second emblem of the sacrament, the water. When flesh is torn, the blood beneath it flows. When the flesh of the Atoning One was torn, it was His atoning blood that flowed. As He said, "I have given [blood] to you upon the altar to make an atonement for your souls: for it is the blood that maketh an atonement for the soul" (Leviticus 17:11).

Receiving the emblems of the sacrament is the key to being founded on the rock of Christ. He is the bread, the torn body that spills the atoning blood, represented by the water. In order to take the sacrament properly, we must be worthy members of the Lord's Church. To become a worthy member of His Church, we must take upon ourselves His name in the waters of baptism and become members of His Church (see Mosiah 18:8–10). We also need to be born of the Spirit (see John 3:5). As His covenant people, we are entitled to have His Spirit with us continually if we always remember Him and keep His commandments. In other words, making, keeping, and renewing covenants through the sacrament are the keys to being founded on the rock of Christ.

The Twelve and the Sacrament

Of note is the fact that 3 Nephi 18 also establishes a pattern that is always to be followed in the Church. The chain of command starts with the Lord; He is the one who gives instructions. We take the sacrament in remembrance of Him. The Savior gave the sacrament to the Twelve first since they are the ones who eat first and become filled (see 3 Nephi 18:1–4). The Twelve then passed the sacrament to the church members (see 3 Nephi 18:5–6). This pattern is critical to follow. If we are to be founded on the rock of Christ, we must follow the counsel given to us from the Twelve. Like the priests in the Mosaic law, the Twelve Apostles are our leaders and stand as intermediaries between us and the Lord.

This is one possible explanation for what the Lord meant when He rebuked Satan by saying "man shall not live by bread alone, but by every word that proceedeth out of the mouth of God" (Matthew 4:4). The bread is the Savior. "Every word that proceedeth out of the mouth of God" comes to us by way of those who are prophets, seers, and revelators. These are the Twelve. In other words, the mere existence of a Savior or our mere membership in His Church, both represented by bread, cannot save us. Instead we must live by "every word" that we receive from the Lord's chosen. We must keep every commandment we are given if we are to live eternally.

Keystones and Cornerstones

The Book of Mormon has been called the keystone of the restored gospel of Jesus Christ. When making this analogy, we usually point out that an arch will crumble if the keystone is taken away. Well, the truth is that an arch is likely to crumble if any stone is taken out of it. The fact that an arch would crumble without any of its other stones actually makes the arch analogy even more appropriate for the entire Church because *all* of the stones in the arch are critical. There would be no restored gospel without revelation, without the priesthood, without temples, without the Relief Society, without the return of Elijah, without a living prophet, and so on. Each of these "stones" is essential to the arch that is the restored gospel of Jesus Christ. Taking out any one of them would cause the entire arch to crumble.

Nevertheless, the Book of Mormon remains the keystone of the Restored Church in a very symbolic manner. You see, when an arch is being constructed, all the stones must be held in place by an external force. But once the keystone is in place, the external supports can be removed. The arch becomes freestanding and self-supporting only after the keystone is in place.

In that respect, the keystone remains a very apt symbol. With the Book of Mormon, the restored gospel is complete, permanent, and self-supporting. The Church does not rely on any external support to stand, as all the necessities of a true and living church are present in the arch itself (see D&C 1:30). The Book of Mormon proves the veracity of Joseph Smith, and the veracity of Joseph Smith proves all other doctrines and facets of the Restoration. Still, it is the keystone—the Book of Mormon—that completes the arch and makes it self-supporting and permanent.

Why would an arch be an appropriate symbol of religion? In architecture—a word that literally contains the word "arch"—an arch can serve two principal functions: a point of entry and a source of support for overhead shelter.

Both of these functions teach of Christ and His Church. The "arch" of the restored Church is not a final destination but is really an entry way to eternity. The Church is the means, not the end. It is the structure through which ordinances and covenants are received and lessons are taught, but its purpose is clearly to lead people to eternity, not to become their final plateau. In this sense, the arch of the restored gospel is an entry point to eternity. Likewise, the arch is a fitting support for eternity. The arch is not the eternal structure itself but is the support for that eternal structure.

This leads to another analogy that the Apostle Paul used to refer to the Savior. "Now therefore ye are no more strangers and foreigners, but fellowcitizens with the saints, and of the household of God; And are built upon the foundation of the apostles and prophets, Jesus Christ himself being the chief corner stone; In whom all the building fitly framed together groweth unto an holy temple in the Lord" (Ephesians 2:19–21).

As President Gordon B. Hinckley noted, "In many instances, including the construction of early temples in the Church, cornerstones were used at each junction point of the walls and put in place with ceremony. The final stone was spoken of as the chief cornerstone, and its placement became the reason for much celebration. With this cornerstone in position, the foundation was ready for the superstructure. Hence the analogy that Paul used in describing the true Church."[5] The Savior is the foundation. With Him in place, the building may proceed.

Rocks and Revelation

At first blush, rocks might seem to hide light or vision, obscuring them instead of giving them. However, many scriptural accounts refer to stones or rocks that reveal truth and light, not obscure them. In the very first chapter of the Book of Mormon, Father Lehi is given a vision that begins with a pillar of fire coming down from above and resting on a rock (see 1 Nephi 1:6). Likewise, Christ referred to the "rock" of revelation given to Peter as the foundation on which His Church was built (see Matthew 16:17–19). In both these examples, rocks are used as the basis for revelation and prophecy. This lesson makes sense when we consider that the testimony of Jesus is the spirit of prophecy (see Revelation 19:10). As we become founded on the Rock and more like the Rock, we find that the veil between ourselves and God becomes thinner. It is by these seer stones that the veil is rent. It is by Christ, the Rock, that the separation between God and man is overcome (see Matthew 27:51).

Formation of Rocks

To understand how stone or rocks are a sure foundation and how we can become founded on the Rock of Christ, it may be helpful to understand the ways in which physical rocks are formed. There are three basic types of rocks on the earth: igneous, sedimentary, and metamorphic.

Igneous rocks are volcanic. They are formed by intense heat or fire. We too may become like the Rock through the refiner's fire, being chosen in the "furnace of affliction" as was Isaiah (Isaiah 48:10). All the suffering, all of the refiner's fire that we experience is for our eternal benefit and serves to make us more like our Father in Heaven (see D&C 122:5–7).

Sedimentary rocks are the next group. They are formed over long periods of time as layers form on top of each other.[6] They are formed "line upon line" in the same way the Lord helps us to grow (see 2 Nephi 28:30; Isaiah 28:10; D&C 128:21). This is the same growth process that the Savior Himself followed, receiving grace for grace (see D&C 93:12–14).

Metamorphic rocks are rocks that are shaped over long periods of time by temperature, pressure, and chemical action.[7] In this process, the rock is under a constant state of refinement. The chief cause of this refinement is that there is water found within the rock. Water, with other forces of nature, helps change the structure of the rock and develop new textural features in it.[8] As we receive more living water, or the words of salvation and the gospel, we also experience a kind of metamorphosis over the course of many years.

Very small or disintegrated rocks are what we call sand. Sand is given in the scriptures to represent hyperbole or a number or quantity beyond comprehension (see Genesis 22:17; 1 Kings 4:20; Revelation 20:8; 1 Nephi 12:1; 20:19; 2 Nephi 20:22; Mormon 1:7; D&C 132:30; Moses 1:28; Abraham 3:14). In this sense, the Lord uses rocks—innumerable tiny rocks—to represent eternity and the blessings of eternal lives (see D&C 132:30).

When sand or rock is exposed to fire or another source of great heat and then experiences rapid cooling, it may form glass.[9] Glass is particularly useful to us since it can be both transparent and translucent. In other words, glass is a wonderful conductor of light. In fact, the earth in its celestial state (the state that denotes the highest degree of light) is called a "sea of glass" (see Revelation 4:6; D&C 77:1).

By no coincidence, the process that forms rocks is also the process that gave the earth its vast supply of water. Volcanic activity not only forms rocks, but it also releases water vapor. This is the source of the water on the earth. Somehow, in a way that may be difficult for us to understand, both water and stone come from the same fountain. The Exodus story illustrated this when Moses smote the rock and water flowed out (see Exodus 17:6). If we find one, we also find the other.

Mountains

Mountains are large formations of rock that are both physically and spiritually closer to God than the rest of the world. A mountain, in simple terms, is a collection of rock layers folded and lifted upwards until it appears to be reaching toward heaven. These rocks, in the form of mountains, have served as places of refuge and revelation, places to receive commandments, places of prayer, and even as the place where the Transfiguration of our Lord occurred. The word "mountain" is often perfectly interchangeable with "temple" in the scriptures.[10] Mountains are literally and symbolically the closest places to heaven on earth, the places where heaven meets earth.

In the language of the Lord, to speak of a mountain is to speak of the temple. A mountain is in essence a huge, God-made rock. As the Savior is the Rock, we see Him typified in His temple. To be founded on the Rock is to be founded on the ordinances and covenants of the mountain of the Lord's house (see Isaiah 2:3; 30:29; Micah 4:1–2).

While visiting Austria many years ago, I learned a symbolic lesson that embodies some of the priceless blessings of the temple. You may be familiar with edelweiss from the classic song in "The Sound of Music." But the story behind edelweiss is much more than a song, even though the song is beautiful. Edelweiss is an extremely rare flower that is a treasure to Austrians. It only grows high on Austrian mountains, far above the noise and pollution of the rest of the world. Because it is so rare and so far beyond the reach of so many people, edelweiss has become a symbol of deep love and affection. Young Austrian men have been known to scale mountains at their own peril to retrieve some edelweiss and present it to the girl of their dreams as a token of their love and devotion. Some brave young Austrian men have even fallen to their deaths in pursuit of some edelweiss to give to their prospective brides. Still they think it worth the risk because nothing is too good or too costly for the girl they love.

While this is not a scriptural symbol, it is still a very appropriate symbolic lesson. Here is the lesson: Young men, if you truly love that young woman, you too will scale the mountain—the mountain of the Lord—to present the girl of your dreams with a priceless token of your undying love—the celestial marriage covenant. This flower is so rare, so beautiful, and so special that it is only found high atop the world, on the Lord's mountain. Unlike the mountains of Austria, the only life that is risked in climbing this mountain is the life of the natural man, the enemy to God (see Mosiah 3:19).

The girl you love is worth any price you may have to pay. You wouldn't dare defile or disgrace such a beautiful and valuable flower, a flower that you'd be willing to risk your life for. Climb that mountain—the temple—and present her with the most beautiful and rare token of your love—the covenant of celestial marriage. And then climb it again and again by returning to the temple throughout all your days to keep the flower blooming.

Altars

Altars express this same symbolic message of mountains on a smaller scale. In this respect, it is much like a temple on a smaller scale. As a raised area stretching toward heaven, an altar is most commonly known as a place of sacrifice. Moses was commanded to build an altar of stones that had not been hewn, or shaped, by the hand of man (see Exodus 20:25; Deuteronomy 27:5). This was to represent that it was the hand of God—not the hand of man—that formed the basis of the sacrifice. Both of these symbolic applications point to the sacrifice of the Lord, which is the center of temple worship.

Summary

As with the earth itself and the water on it, rocks are another essential material that points to Christ. There would be no earth or life on earth without rocks. The strength, many uses, omnipresence, and even formation of rocks all teach us profound lessons of the Savior.

Deuteronomy talks of an apostate people whose "rock is not our Rock" (Deuteronomy 32:31). If we will build on the foundation of the Rock, we are promised that the adversary will not prevail (see Helaman 5:12). That is what rock represents and what it means to be built on the Rock of Christ and receive the blessings that come from the most solid of foundations.

Notes

1. *Webster's New World Dictionary, College Edition* (Cleveland: The World Publishing Company, 1962), 1282.
2. Strong, *Strong's Exhaustive Concordance of the Bible*, Hebrew word 1035.
3. Joseph Fielding McConkie & Donald W. Parry, *A Guide to Scriptural Symbols*, (Salt Lake City: Bookcraft, 1990), 25.
4. See also Paul's comparison of the Church to the body of Christ in Ephesians 4:11–13; 5:23–30.
5. Gordon B. Hinckley, "Four Cornerstones of Faith," *Ensign*, February, 2004, 2–7.
6. Hamblin, *The Earth's Dynamic Systems*, 94.
7. Ibid., 116.
8. Ibid., 120.
9. Ibid., 72–73.
10. McConkie & Parry, *A Guide to Scriptural Symbols*, 84–85.

Trees

In one of the next periods of creation, the Creator was careful to place all manner of plant life throughout the earth, including, and perhaps most prominently, trees (see Genesis 1:11–12).

Even in the desert, trees are present. They embody life. Trees grow tall, dwarfing their surroundings and reaching majestically toward heaven. Even if they grow on an inclined or slanted surface, they still reach straight up toward the sun. Many of them bear fruit throughout their lives. They often outlive man. They give us beautiful wood. They give shade from the heat. Food, clothing, and shelter—the basic necessities of mortal survival—can all be had abundantly from trees. These physical observations also carry spiritual lessons, and it is no coincidence that the Lord has chosen trees to teach many spiritual lessons in the scriptures.

Trees in the Scriptures

Generally speaking, trees are used in the scriptures to symbolize righteous men.[1] While the earth itself, light, water, and rock point directly to Christ, the work of the next creative period points symbolically toward God's greatest creation: man. Specifically, trees are used to represent the righteousness that men can achieve on earth.

The first Psalm uses the imagery of a tree beautifully to represent and contrast righteous and unrighteous men.

> Blessed is the man that walketh not in the counsel of the ungodly,

> nor standeth in the way of sinners, nor sitteth in the seat of the scornful.
>
> But his delight is in the law of the Lord; and in his law doth he meditate day and night.
>
> And he shall be like a tree planted by the rivers of water, that bringeth forth his fruit in his season; his leaf also shall not wither; and whatsoever he doeth shall prosper.
>
> The ungodly are not so: but are like the chaff which the wind driveth away. (Psalms 1:1–4)

As noted by the psalmist, trees stand firm, undaunted by winds or opposition. They are planted firmly and draw their nourishment from water, which is often used to represent the word of God or an emblem of covenant (see Moses 6:60). Those who stand firm in the gospel likewise draw their strength from the word of God and from making and keeping gospel covenants. In contrast, the "ungodly" (unrighteous men) draw no such support from water but are vulnerable to the elements like "chaff."

The Savior also used trees in teaching how to discern a true prophet from a false prophet:

> Beware of false prophets, which come to you in sheep's clothing, but inwardly they are ravening wolves.
>
> Ye shall know them by their fruits. Do men gather grapes of thorns, or figs of thistles?
>
> Even so every good tree bringeth forth good fruit; but a corrupt tree bringeth forth evil fruit.
>
> A good tree cannot bring forth evil fruit, neither can a corrupt tree bring forth good fruit.
>
> Every tree that bringeth not forth good fruit is hewn down, and cast into the fire.
>
> Wherefore by their fruits ye shall know them. (Matthew 7:15–20)

Here again, both righteous and unrighteous men are depicted by trees. Righteous men are described as bearing good fruit, while corrupt men bring evil fruit. Contrasting this scripture with Psalms 1:1–4, we note that righteous men draw their strength from rivers of water, which they use to produce good fruit and resist withering.

In paying tribute to Joseph and Hyrum Smith, John Taylor compared them to "green trees" in and through whom water flowed (D&C 135:6). On the other hand, corrupt men are the opposite of green trees. They are "dry," far away from rivers (see Luke 23:31). They are good only to be cast into the fire at the day of judgment (see Alma 5:52; Jacob 5:77).

In Lehi's vision, the Lord illustrated the destination of the righteous as a beautiful tree bearing a fruit more desirable than any other (see 1 Nephi 8). This tree was the goal of the righteous because its fruit was so wonderful. The fruit of this particular tree symbolized the love of God (see 1 Nephi 11:25).

Alma also uses the symbolism of a tree by teaching us to develop our faith like a seed that it may grow as a tree (see Alma 32:28–43). Using this imagery, a seed may become as majestic as a tree with the application of the first principle of the gospel: faith in the Lord Jesus Christ.

Malachi uses trees to illustrate the concept of an eternal family (see Malachi 4:1–6). He compares the children of God to trees when he teaches us how to avoid being left without "root" or "branch." In this case, our roots are our forefathers, and our branches are our descendants. The sealing power held by and restored through Elijah (see D&C 110) is the power to keep the family tree—roots, branches, and all—intact throughout eternity. Just as we may not be saved without our ancestors, a tree that somehow loses access to its roots will quickly wither and die. Likewise, even with its roots intact, a tree with no branches is still called a stump.

Similar to Malachi's symbolism, Isaiah uses "root" and "stem"—both elements of a tree—to prophesy of Christ and the great prophets of the last days (see Isaiah 11:1–5; D&C 113:1–6).

Israel's blessing of Joseph likens Joseph unto "a fruitful bough, even a fruitful bough by the well; whose branches run over the wall" (Genesis 49:22). In addition to fulfilling the Abrahamic Covenant, this metaphor is a reference to Joseph's seed, who would "run over the wall" and populate the Book of Mormon lands through Joseph's own "branch," Lehi.

Trees in the Garden of Eden

In the Garden of Eden, we see two trees: the tree of knowledge of good and evil and the tree of life. In the first tree, we see the elements of mortality. In the second tree, we see the elements of immortality and eternal life. These two concepts are the sum and substance of the meaning of life. They represent man's mortal status and his immortal potential. Both concepts are conveyed through the use of trees.

Since many other scriptures use trees to describe righteous men, these two trees may likewise be linked with righteous men. In the tree of knowledge of good and evil, we see not just mortality, but a representation of the righteous man who ushered in mortality: Adam. In the tree of life, we see not just immortality and the love of God, but the righteous man who ushers in immortality and personifies the love of God: Jesus Christ. In a very real sense, Christ is the tree of life.

Mortality and the Tree of Knowledge

The tree of knowledge of good and evil is inseparably connected with mortality. It was the act of eating the fruit from this tree that brought about mortality (see 2 Nephi 2:19–20). The story connected with this tree includes some of mortality's most prominent traits, such as blaming. "The woman who thou gavest to be with me, she gave me of the tree, and I did eat," blamed Adam (Genesis 3:12). Eve further passed the blame: "The serpent beguiled me" (Genesis 3:13). The fruit of the tree of knowledge of good and evil also brought about sweat, sorrow, thorns, thistles, and a destiny to return to the dust of the earth—in other words, to suffer physical death (see Genesis 3:16–19).

However, it's not all bad, by any means. Eating the fruit of the tree brought us here to earth (see 2 Nephi 2:21–24). Without this act, there would be no human family. The fruit of this tree made it possible for us to live and live joyfully at that (see 2 Nephi 2:25). Further, in order to help us through our existence, the Lord placed "enmity"—a protection—between us and the adversary (see Genesis 3:15). This enmity leaves us with a vulnerable heel, but the adversary is left with an unprotected head (see Genesis 3:15). As children of Adam and Eve, we are much better off with only a weak heel as opposed to a weak head. We actually have power over the adversary because of this enmity.

Mortality is the fruit of the tree of knowledge of good and evil, the tree of Adam. With the sweat, sorrow, life, rejoicing and ever-present opposition that resulted from this fruit, we have the perfect summary of mortality. Yes, it is difficult and inevitably painful, but it's also wonderful. While mortality is necessarily rough, it is still *life*. And life is a divine gift to be treasured. In mortality we too will inevitably fall just like Adam and Eve. But, with the help of a Redeemer, we can get back up.

Jesus Christ as the Tree of Life

In the Lord's plan, the fruit of the first tree leads us to the fruit of the second tree: the tree of life. "Trees can be representative of men, but the tree of life typifies the greatest Man of all—the Son of God."[2] Whether it is a sample of the love of God as represented in Lehi's vision or the fulness of that love in His actual presence, the tree of life represents the Savior Himself. Adam brought mortality through the fruit of the tree of knowledge, and the second Adam—Jesus Christ—brings immortality and eternal life through the fruit of the tree of life (see 1 Corinthians 15:44–48).

The Link between the Two Trees

We have all partaken of the fruit of the tree of knowledge of good and evil, since we are in mortality. This fruit would be most bitter if not for the prospect of eating the fruit of the tree of life. While we are enduring the consequences of mortality and the fruit of the tree of knowledge, we look forward to eating from the tree of life.

As is common with other scriptural references to trees, these two trees both represent men. The first represents man as he is, and the second represents man as he may become (see 3 Nephi 12:48; 27:27). Jesus Christ, the key to man reaching his eternal potential, is also represented in the tree of life (see John 14:6).

Of all the lines Lucifer could have fed Eve to tempt her into eating the forbidden fruit, he chose to appeal to her desire to become more godlike. He told her simply that eating of that fruit would make her and Adam "as gods, knowing good and evil" (Genesis 3:5). For all we know, he might have tried before, using completely different temptations. What we do know, however, is that this was the enticement that worked.

Eve did eat of the tree of knowledge and convinced Adam to share the fruit with her (see Genesis 3:6–7). Their eyes were immediately opened, and mortality was ushered in, making life possible for the whole human race (see Genesis 3:6; 2 Nephi 2:20).

Volumes of commentary have been written about this event. Many incorrectly view it as a catastrophe that has brought automatic sin upon every child born into this world. This is in large part because they fail to see the link between the two trees and their symbolic meanings. The doctrine of the Fall is not depressing at all when it is in viewed in light of the doctrine of redemption through the Messiah. On this subject, the Prophet Joseph Fielding Smith taught:

> It may seem very cruel to us without any understanding of all the circumstances, to know that the Fall brought upon us all such awful consequences, and made it possible for an infinite atonement to be offered to amend the broken law. Adam and Eve did not come here in a mortal state. They had to come in the manner in which they did and then transgress the law. The transgression of that law, contrary to the view of many, was not a sin. It was not a sin any more than the transgression in the laboratory by a chemist in combining two substances and creating another entirely different from the first. It was not a sin to bring to pass mortality, a condition which was essential to the eternal welfare of man. The Fall changed the nature of Adam and Eve to fit them for the condition in which we now are. After the coming of an angel with the plan of salvation informing Adam and Eve of the redemption which was to be made by Jesus Christ, Eve rejoiced and said: "Were it not for our transgressions we never should have had seed, and never should have known good and evil, and the joy of our redemption, and the eternal life which God giveth unto all the obedient" (Moses 5:11).
>
> All of this had come because of the Fall. Yes, it was "inevitable"; it had to be . . . . There may be some things that we have to accept on faith, and we should prepare ourselves to accept all things which the Lord reveals, whether we fully understand them or not.[3]

My twelve-year-old daughter once asked for a little help in understanding the relationship between the two trees. She was wondering how Adam's "transgression"—in which he acted against a commandment of God—could be a positive thing.

I responded, "Kayla, let's say you had a bad accident. Let's say you were cut badly, so badly that you would bleed to death if you weren't treated immediately. I would want to get you to the hospital as soon as possible, and you would want me to do that, wouldn't you?"

She heartily agreed.

"Now, I would be the first to admit that I would break the speed limit to get you to the hospital quickly. You would want me to do that, wouldn't you?"

Again, she heartily agreed.

"Now, let's suppose that because I hurried so much to get you to the hospital in time, you ended up being fine. But on the way there, I broke the law by speeding, didn't I?"

Again, she agreed.

"But did I sin?"

Her face lit up, and the lesson was clear. Yes, a law was transgressed, but the result was life. Without question, the greater law was served, and the purposes of God were advanced not just in spite of the transgression but *because* of the transgression. In this case, transgressing one law (eating of the first fruit) is not catastrophic as long as we are heading toward the Great Healer. Understanding that the fruit of the first tree gives us access to the fruit of the second tree makes the once-bitter fruit much sweeter.

The Symbolism behind the Two Trees

Again, trees generally represent people—withered trees represent unrighteous people (see Matthew 13:6; John 15:6; Jude 1:12; Jacob 5:40, 45) and healthy trees represent righteous people (see D&C 135:6). Those same analogies carry lessons for us in examining our own mortal state and progressing from one tree to the other.

In the Garden of Eden, both trees actually represent righteous men. Notice that even after they had eaten from the tree of knowledge of good and evil and were cast out of the Garden of Eden, Adam and Eve were still facing eastward—a holy direction.[4] Contrary to the perception held by most of the Christian world, Adam and Eve were still literally headed in the right direction after the Fall. Notice also that nothing in the scriptures suggests that the tree of knowledge of good and evil wilted or died, as a tree representing an unrighteous man would be expected to do.

This is because the tree of knowledge of good and evil—typified by Adam—is truly a tree of righteousness, not unrighteousness. The natural man may be an enemy to God (Mosiah 3:19), but he is also a son of God who is "a little lower than the angels" (Hebrews 2:7). And a son of God is intended to grow to be like *the* Son of God (see 3 Nephi 12:48; 27:27), who is personified by the tree of life.

The differences between the trees are not irreconcilable. Through the Atonement of Christ, Adam (meaning all mortal men and women) can be brought into harmony with God. The fruit of the tree of knowledge of good and evil is hardly bitter at all as long as we look forward to the fruit of the tree of life. Adam (represented by the tree of knowledge of good and evil) can find infinite happiness, joy and even godliness in Christ (represented by the tree of life). The fruit of mortality can in reality make us like Gods as long as we partake of the fruit of the tree of life through the covenants and ordinances of the restored gospel (see Alma 5:62).

This is exactly what the Savior taught His disciples shortly before He was betrayed: "Verily, verily I say unto you, That ye shall weep and lament, but the world shall rejoice: and ye shall be sorrowful, but your sorrow shall be turned into joy. A woman when she is in travail hath sorrow, because her hour is come: but as soon as she is delivered of the child, she remembereth no more the anguish, for joy that a man is born into the world" (John 16:20–21). Looking to the tree of life turns the fruit of mortality into the joyful fruit of immortality. Eating from this tree takes away the painful taste of the fruit of the other tree.

The Lord most appropriately chose trees as the instrument through which mortality and experience, the seeds of godliness and godhood, were brought to us.

The Cross on Calvary: Trees and the Atonement

Of all the scriptural references to trees, there is one tree in particular that stands out to all of Christianity. It is the tree or cross on which our Lord was crucified. "The God of our fathers raised up Jesus, whom ye slew and hanged on a tree" (Acts 5:30). A tree was the medium of the great and last sacrifice of the Lord (see Alma 34:13). When we consider the eternal life that comes from this infinite sacrifice, the symbol of death on Calvary actually becomes yet another depiction of the tree of life—of eternal life.

In the Garden of Eden, we saw trees as the two "bookends" of mortality: knowledge of good and evil (or mortality) and life (immortality and eternal life). These trees mark the necessary steps to fulfilling the Father's plan whereby His children inherit exaltation. On Golgotha we see another tree that makes the blessings of eternal life and exaltation possible. This sacrifice is the archetype that all other sacrifices follow.

One of the very first actions recorded in the scriptures is Adam's offering of the firstlings of his flocks as a representation of the sacrifice of the Savior.

> And after many days an angel of the Lord appeared unto Adam, saying: Why dost thou offer sacrifices unto the Lord? And Adam said unto him: I know not, save the Lord commanded me.
>
> And then the angel spake, saying: This thing is a similitude of the sacrifice of the Only Begotten of the Father, which is full of grace and truth.
>
> Wherefore, thou shalt do all that thou doest in the name of the Son, and thou shalt repent and call upon God in the name of the Son forevermore. (Moses 5:6–8)

Just like Adam and Eve, we are commanded to make sacrifices in similitude of the sacrifice of our Lord and Savior. The word "sacrifice" comes from the Latin *sacerficium*, which contains two basic roots. They are *sacer*, which means "sacred," and *facere*, which means "to make."[5] In other words, sacrifice means to make holy or sacred. It is basically a synonym of "sanctify," which has almost the same Latin roots: *sanctus*, meaning "sacred or holy" and *facere*. Sacrifice is also commonly associated in English with giving up something. When we repent and come unto Christ as a little child (see 3 Nephi 9:22), our hearts are made sacred or holy. Again, this purification or sanctification is made possible only through the sacrifice of Jesus.

Anciently, in the Mosaic instructions of sacrifice, there were two basic elements. One was the sacrifice itself, often a lamb or the firstborn and finest of the flock; this obviously was in similitude of the Firstborn, the Lamb of God. The second thing was "wood for the burnt offering" (Genesis 22:3). Wood was included, just as the sacrifice itself, to draw us back to Christ and the wood on which He was sacrificed.

The burning of the sacrifice brings to mind not just the Savior, but also one of His specific missions. When John the Baptist prepared the way for the Savior, he preached of one infinitely mightier than he who would baptize with fire and with the Holy Ghost (see Matthew 3:11). Christ is the promised Savior to "purify with fire."[6] Fire is the great refiner; it purges dross and impurities and leaves a purified and beautiful product. This is a moving illustration of what the Atonement does for us.

Isaiah described part of the Messiah's mission as giving "beauty for ashes" (Isaiah 61:3). After the covenant of baptism and taking upon ourselves the name of Christ, we are given the gift of the Holy Ghost. Only in this way may we have our impurities and ungodliness burned from us and turned to ashes, symbolically speaking. We sacrifice our natural-man hearts for a new life in the footsteps of the Savior. In doing so, we will receive "beauty for ashes"—holiness for the sacrifice we make in similitude of the Savior's. In that light, the elements of wood and burning are tied directly to the sacrifice of our Lord and Savior.

In summary, that great and ultimate sacrifice wrought on a tree made salvation and eternal life possible by the purging or burning away of imperfections.

The Cross and the Temple

A cross carries a deeper symbolic meaning in its very form. A cross is basically a union of two pieces of wood, one horizontal piece and one vertical piece. The sign of the cross is formed when the two pieces are brought together, although the vertical piece is more prominent.

This "intersection" is suggested in the definition of a temple, as noted by Hugh Nibley.[7] The two intersecting lines represent the joining of God (the vertical line—think of a steeple on a temple pointing straight up, drawing our eyes and minds toward heaven) and man (the horizontal line). This explanation provides a very fitting definition of a temple, as man and God are brought into harmony through the ordinances of the temple. Their wills intersect and are joined through the covenants of the temple.

This is likewise a fitting representation of the Atonement. Christ's suffering in Gethsemane and death on the wooden cross are the basis for the temple ordinances and blessings. Man and God are brought into harmony through the Atonement, and the Atonement is fully accessed only through the ordinances of the temple.

The Stick of Judah and the Stick of Joseph

> Take thee one stick, and write upon it, For Judah, and for the children of Israel his companions: then take another stick, and write upon it, For Joseph, the stick of Ephraim, and for all the house of Israel his companions:
>
> And join them one to another into one stick; and they shall become one in thine hand.
>
> Thus saith the Lord God; Behold, I will take the stick of Joseph,

> which is in the hand of Ephraim, and the tribes of Israel his fellows, and will put them with him, even with the stick of Judah, and make them one stick, and they shall be one in my hand. (Ezekiel 37:16, 17, 19)

We are familiar with this scripture as a biblical reference to the Book of Mormon. The word "stick" in this text is the Hebrew *ets* or *ates*, which literally means "wood" or "tree."[8] In this scripture, we see trees used as the method of conveying the word of God. When we consider that "the Word" is another name for Jesus (John 1:1), we can also appreciate how the wood or tree on which He was crucified "conveyed" the Word. His sacrifice was wrought on that tree and is now taught through the "trees" or "sticks" of Judah and Ephraim.

Building with Wood

The role of wood in mortality does not end with the cross of the crucifixion or the medium for conveying the word of God. With wood from trees, Noah built an ark (see Genesis 8), the Jaredites built barges (see Ether 2), and Nephi built a ship (see 1 Nephi 17, 18). These wooden vessels all carried their occupants across the water to lands free from the sin and persecution that had surrounded them. Each of these faithful groups left behind crumbling apostate societies with the indispensable help of wood. Our method of symbolically accomplishing the same also relies on the wood of the Atonement and the scriptures.

Wood is used not only to build ships, but also to erect houses. Houses also have many symbolic applications. The Lord refers to His covenant people as "the House of Israel." Wise men who follow the example of the Savior build their "house" on the Rock. All latter-day temples bear the inscription, "The House of the Lord." The home, a close synonym to "house," is the second most sacred place on earth, behind only the temple.

Throughout history, wood has been essential to building shelters. Picture, if you can, life as we know it without wood for a building material. Not much comes to mind, does it? Without wood buildings, we would certainly be limited. Even great stone buildings like the Salt Lake temple rely heavily on wooden frameworks, both inside the structure and outside the structure while it is under construction. Without wood, we might possibly have some buildings made purely of stone, but even the great stone pyramids could not have been built without the use of wood to build the scaffolds and pulleys that lifted the stones in place.

Building anything with wood also requires something else to fasten and hold the pieces of wood together. Throughout world history, two principal things have been used to do this—lashings and nails. We recognize these as the emblems of the crucifixion. Christ was scourged, or whipped with lashings (see Matthew 27:26). Then, with unmeasured cruelty, He was nailed to the cross (see Matthew 27:35).

While the enemies of Christ used lashings, nails, and wood to take life, those same tokens give life through the Atonement. "Surely he hath borne our griefs, and carried our sorrows . . . But he was wounded for our transgressions, and bruised for our iniquities: the chastisement of our peace was upon him; and with his stripes we are healed" (Isaiah 53:4–5).

If we are to build an earthly dwelling, we have to make good use of wood, lashings, and nails. If we are to build any kind of eternal dwelling, we likewise have to make good use of the wood and nails of the cross and the lashings inflicted on our Lord. These building materials are far too precious for us to waste.

The Creation

Following the Creation accounts in the books of Genesis, Moses, and Abraham, on the third day, the earth was prepared to bring forth trees, grass, and all manner of plant life (see Genesis 1:11–13; Moses 2:11–13; Abraham 4:11–13). The fact that this occurred on the third day is especially significant because the number three is found throughout the accounts of the Atonement. There were three crosses on Calvary (see Luke 23:32). Three hours of darkness accompanied the events on Calvary (see Luke 23:44). The Book of Mormon records that earthquakes and terrible storms persisted for three hours after the crucifixion (see 3 Nephi 8:19). Three days of darkness then covered the land when the Light of the World was taken (see 3 Nephi 8:23). Finally, Christ was resurrected on the third day (see Mosiah 3:10). All of these examples—even the Creation period in which trees were planted on earth—draw us back to Christ and His Atonement.

Eternity

We were probably all taught something special about trees when we were very young. We were taught that if we could see the cross-section of a tree trunk, we could tell how old it was by counting the rings. These tree rings are also a great illustration of eternity. The circles all have the same center, but they don't have a beginning or an ending point. The scriptures often mention "one eternal round" in reference to the Lord's ways (see 1 Nephi 10:19; Alma 37:12; D&C 3:2).

Like tree rings, the rings that we wear as tokens of an eternal marriage covenant are circular and without beginning or end. Although our finite minds are stuck thinking in terms of years, the Lord works in terms of eternity. In a tree we see both time and eternity: The rings each represent a year of growth, and yet their design—with no beginning or end—illustrates eternity.

I remember looking at tree rings and being reminded of a diagram of our solar system. The planets are depicted in their orbit by rings of different sizes just like the tree rings. The interesting thing about tree rings is that no matter how big or small the rings are, or even if they're not perfectly round, they all have the same center. More specifically, they all revolve around the same central object. So it is with the solar system. The planets have varying orbits, but they all revolve around one thing: the sun. Likewise, all eternity revolves around the Son of God.

A Source of Life

Just like the Savior, trees and other plants are the agents of a life-sustaining process on earth called photosynthesis. The tree takes in harmful carbon-dioxide along with water and light from the sun and converts those substances to oxygen and carbohydrates (food)—both agents essential to life. The substance within plants that makes the whole process possible is a pigment called chlorophyll, which is also what gives plants their green color. Green is a particularly symbolic color, representing life and fertility. Through photosynthesis, trees (and other plants) preserve our lives by giving us the oxygen necessary for us to survive. Trees make use of water and light to purge harmful substances and somehow exchange them for life. By the same token, only the Savior's Atonement can exchange purity for sin, life for death, or beauty for ashes (see Isaiah 61:3).

The Four Seasons

Perhaps few things on this earth reflect the four seasons as well as trees. Like trees, the four seasons themselves typify Christ. Because the seasons are cyclical, or circular, like eternity, we can't really pick out a beginning or an end. Once again, the temporal teaches us the eternal.

Summer is the time when trees are the most green and beautiful. The sun is shining brightly, and the trees proudly display their fruit. This is the harvest time, given for us to save our souls (see Jeremiah 8:20; D&C 56:16). This is also the time when the waters of Jordan, the waters in which the Savior was baptized, "overflow" (Joshua 3:15). The ant, a symbol of industriousness, "Provideth her meat in the summer, and gathereth her food in the harvest" (Proverbs 6:8). Summer is also given as the time of the Second Coming of the Savior (see Matthew 24:32; Mark 13:28; Luke 21:30; D&C 35:16; 45:37; JS Matthew 1:38). In short, summer is the time to get work done.

Fall and winter follow, typifying death or apostasy. In these seasons many trees lose their adornments as their leaves fall to the earth. The trees then go bare. The earth is at an angle relative to the sun that doesn't allow as much warmth to reach it. It is a cold season.

Spring follows victoriously, and life returns. We celebrate the Resurrection of Christ in the spring. We are taught that His birth was actually in the spring (see D&C 20:1). Spring is a period of great happenings and beginnings in the Church. Joseph Smith received the First Vision in the spring. The Church was organized in the spring. The prophet Elijah returned in the spring, restoring the keys to the fulness of the Priesthood (see D&C 110). We meet as a general Church body in the spring for General Conference. In the springtime many trees blossom and prepare to bear their fruit.

And then the cycle of life begins again with the new season, and once again trees mark the ongoing seasons of mortality.

Fire

Wood has provided a source of fire and warmth throughout history. As with other gospel symbols, fire can be a positive force or a destructive force. Fire that is uncontained and unwelcome destroys both property and life (see Malachi 4:1; Matthew 3:12; Revelation 8:7; D&C 64:23). In this sense, the negative applications of fire may be symbolic of approaching the Lord unworthily or overstepping the bounds the Lord has set.

On the other hand, when fire is contained and used properly within the Lord's plan, it only destroys what is not wanted or needed (see Isaiah 1:25; Hebrews 1:3; 9:22; 2 Nephi 16:6–7; D&C 43:11; 128:24). While it certainly can be destructive, the intended and symbolic use of fire is to provide purification, light, and warmth. These are the same functions of Christ and the blessings of the Holy Ghost that flow from His sacrifice.

Other Lessons from Trees

Understanding that healthy trees generally represent righteous people, there are at least a few more lessons to be learned from them. The strongest trees that withstand the most fearsome storms and tests of time are generally the ones with the strongest root structure. Just look at a giant sequoia, a California redwood, a towering ponderosa pine, or the famous cedars of Lebanon. The root structure of these great trees is a lesson on strengthening our spiritual roots in the gospel. It may also be a lesson in strengthening family relations and performing temple work, as the Lord has compared our "roots" to our forefathers (see Malachi 4:1). The stronger the roots, the stronger the tree. If we want to grow, we should start by strengthening our roots.

However, if you've ever noticed a palm tree, you may learn another lesson on withstanding storms. In the Arizona desert, palm trees are very common. They can grow very high and can live many years, lining many streets for decades in the Phoenix area. These trees withstand some fierce and sometimes violent storms in the area. In fact, in all the years I've lived in the area, I don't think I've ever seen a palm tree downed by a storm.

However, their structure is the exact opposite of a California redwood or other seemingly indestructible trees. Their root structure is tiny, barely extending beyond the trunk of the tree and only going a few feet further into the ground. I've often wondered how such a relatively shallow-rooted plant could survive.

Well, palm trees illustrate that there is more than one way to withstand the most ferocious of storms, and in doing so grow strong, tall, and venerable. The palm tree does it by being extremely flexible and aerodynamic. A palm tree is not bulky. It doesn't give the storm much to grab on to. Like water on a duck, storms roll right off a palm tree because the tree is thin and flexible. For lack of a better term, the palm tree is very forgiving.

In this sense, palm trees embody many of the characteristics of charity. "And charity suffereth long, and is kind, and envieth not, and is not puffed up, seeketh not her own, is not easily provoked, thinketh no evil, and rejoiceth not in inquity but rejoiceth in the truth, beareth all things, believeth all things, hopeth all things, endureth all things" (Moroni 7:45).

We could learn a great deal from the structure of palm trees. Unfortunately, there are far too many members of the Church who are seeking to grow strong and tall like a redwood but who become offended and unnecessarily affected by storms. In their quest to become trees of righteousness, they are sometimes quick to take offense, even at little things. Often these people carry unnecessary loads because they are quickly offended and slow to forgive. This makes it very difficult for them to grow and endure and become trees of righteousness since all that extra baggage makes them easy prey for a storm that wouldn't even faze a flexible, sleek palm tree.

Likewise, there are others who are overly rigid and refuse to compromise, even over little things. These people just have to be right. This rigidity can snap them like a twig, while a flexible palm tree barely even notices such problems.

Comparing trees to righteous men, we would do well to follow the examples of both the strong-rooted giants and the palm trees. Our roots must be strong, deep, and wide to grow and endure. At the same time, it takes years for roots to deepen and expand. During those years while we are deepening and nourishing our roots, we should follow the example of the palm tree, learning to repent and forgive, not to take offense easily, and to be easily approachable. After all, these are characteristics of a charitable follower of Christ.

Summary

Near the beginning of His earthly ministry, the Savior quoted Isaiah to proclaim His divinity in the synagogue in Nazareth (see Luke 4:16–21) The scripture quoted by the Savior explains the Savior's mission quite well, again using trees as the example. The Lord was sent "To appoint unto them that mourn in Zion, to give unto them beauty for ashes, the oil of joy for mourning, the garment of praise for the spirit of heaviness; that they might be called *trees of righteousness, the planting of the Lord,* that he might be glorified" (Isaiah 61:3, emphasis added).

Among the countless spiritual and eternal lessons from trees, perhaps the central message is that our becoming "trees of righteousness" depends on the Savior and the tree of His sacrifice.

Notes

1. McConkie & Parry, *A Guide to Scriptural Symbols*, 103–04.
2. Ibid., 104.
3. Joseph Fielding Smith, *Answers to Gospel Questions*, vol. 2, (Salt Lake City: Deseret Book, 1958), 214–15.
4. Alonzo L. Gaskill, *The Savior & The Serpent* (Salt Lake City: Shadow Mountain, 2005), 180.
5. *Webster's New World Dictionary, College Edition* (The World Publishing Company, 1962).
6. *Hymns of the Church of Jesus Christ of Latter-day Saints* (Salt Lake City: Intellectual Reserve, 1985), no. 175.
7. Nibley, *Mormonism and Early Christianity*, 358.
8. Strong, *Strong's Exhaustive Concordance of the Bible,* Hebrew word 6086.
   See also the footnote from Ezekiel 37 in the LDS Bible which teaches that, "Wooden writing tablets were in common use in Babylon in Ezekiel's day."

Matter and Energy

Far too many people have paved their own spiritual and intellectual dead ends by attempting to replace God in their understanding of the Creation. Rather than acknowledging the Creation as the work of Divinity, they see it as an infinite coincidence and the product of chance. Those who view the universe as a concoction of chance have often tried to use the findings of science to explain away the existence of God. What a miserable pursuit. With this view, they must necessarily see life as a tunnel that leads nowhere. However, if we open our spiritual eyes, hearts, and minds and explore the tunnel of mortality, we can learn more about the universe and the principles that govern it, and we will find that the tunnel has no end. In reality, the tunnel is a gateway to immortality and to God. The findings of science that line the walls of this tunnel of mortality should serve to strengthen our belief in God, not to nullify our belief in Him. One of the most brilliant and revered scientists of all, Albert Einstein, understood this. He remarked, "I want to know God's thoughts; the rest are details."[1]

Matter

Science accepts that matter cannot be created or destroyed. From this truth we learn a lesson on eternity. The Prophet Joseph Smith confirmed that "the elements are eternal. That which has a beginning will surely have an end."[2] He also taught, "The pure principles of element are principles which can never be destroyed; they may be organized and re-organized, but not destroyed. They had no beginning, and they can have no end."[3]

Spirit also abides by these same laws of matter. It too is without beginning or end, since it is also matter. "There is no such thing as immaterial matter. All spirit is matter, but it is more fine or pure, and can only be discerned by purer eyes; We cannot see it; but when our bodies are purified we shall see that it is all matter" (D&C 131:7–8).

These fundamentals are important and point to Christ because they dispel two popular untruths. The first untruth that is dispelled is the atheist's point of view. An atheist who believes that life is finite and that there is no afterlife is ignoring the truths of eternity and of science. He is imagining the possibility of simply popping into existence one day and popping out when physical death comes. Eternity is real, as matter testifies. The atheist who succeeds in convincing himself that life ends with physical death will have quite a shock when he discovers that his spirit, like the elements, is eternal.

The other untruth disarmed by the nature of matter is the apostate notion of ex-nihilism, or that God created the world from nothing. Joseph Smith once again clarified this for us.

> You ask the learned doctors why they say the world was made out of nothing; and they will answer, "Doesn't the Bible say He created the world?" And they infer, from the word create, that it must have been made out of nothing. Now, the word create came from the word *barau* which does not mean to create out of nothing; it means to organize; the same as a man would organize materials and build a ship. Hence, we infer that God had materials to organize the world out of chaos—chaotic matter, which is element, and in which dwells all the glory.[4]

Energy

Like matter, energy cannot be created nor destroyed. Energy is defined as power, or in physics it is the capacity to do work or overcome resistance. If anything is to get done, energy is necessary. Energy, whether in the form of heat or electric current, always follows a distinct pattern in flowing from a concentration of greater energy to a concentration of lesser energy until a state of equilibrium is reached. This is the same way that we receive all of our energy, light, and truth. It comes from a greater concentration (Deity) to a lesser concentration (us).

Remember that equilibrium is the goal in this flow of energy. The goal of God the Father and His Son is "to bring to pass the immortality and eternal life of man" (Moses 1:39). If we follow the methods and path outlined by the laws of God, we will attain this equilibrium and become heirs to "all that [the] Father hath" (D&C 84:38). Like Abraham, Isaac, and Jacob, we will become not angels but gods (see D&C 132:37). Our Father in Heaven wants nothing more than for us to have the same blessings of exaltation that He enjoys.

The interesting thing about this process of becoming more like God is that the Father, in giving, loses nothing. Instead He gains all the more from our progress. Our progress glorifies Him (see Moses 1:39). Like the greatest source of energy in our realm—the sun—God is glorified and His effects become more pronounced the more He gives. More specifically, since He is always giving, God is glorified the more He is received.

Equilibrium

If the universe were in a perfect state of equilibrium, no work could be done. There would be no greater or lesser concentration, so no energy would flow. A universe in equilibrium would be a dead universe. Perhaps this kind of universe is what Satan proposed when he sought to take away man's agency. To keep us alive and growing, we rely on the flow of energy, perhaps better stated as blessings or righteousness, to flow from the greater concentration (God) to us, the lesser concentration. The lesson here is that we should not disrupt this flow of righteousness so that our lives can always be maintained. Without agency, this flow would be cut off.

The base for the word "equilibrium" is the Latin "aequus," which means "even" or "equal."[5] The English word "equity" also stems from this word and is similar in meaning. Following this Latin meaning of the word, the opposite of "equity" is "iniquity."[6] This is the familiar word defined by Webster's as "lack of righteousness or justice; wickedness; sin."[7] In this sense, a state of equilibrium would be a state without sin. As equilibrium is the natural course and goal of energy, it is also the natural spiritual course and goal in the plan of salvation.

However, it is the process of reaching that equilibrium in the spiritual sense that is essential to our existence. For our mortal purposes, an equilibrium mortality or a mortality without opposition to righteousness would indeed be a dead world since it would give us no growth.

> For it must needs be, that there is an opposition in all things. If not so, my first-born in the wilderness, righteousness could not be brought to pass, neither wickedness, neither holiness nor misery, neither good nor bad. Wherefore, all things must needs be a compound in one; wherefore, if it should be one body it must needs remain as dead, having no life neither death, nor corruption nor incorruption, happiness nor misery, neither sense nor insensibility.
>
> Wherefore, it must needs have been created for a thing of naught; wherefore there would have been no purpose in the end of its creation. Wherefore, this thing must needs destroy the wisdom of God and his eternal purposes, and also the power, and the mercy, and the justice of God. (2 Nephi 2:11–12)

Without opposites or opposition, this would be a dead world. Energy would not flow; nobody would progress. As Lehi taught, the purpose of God would be completely frustrated since we know that we were created to gain eternal life and immortality (see Moses 1:39). Opposition makes all work and growth possible, both temporally and spiritually. While we are in mortality and learning to be more like our Savior and Father in Heaven, we rely on the laws of equilibrium to sustain us with a flow of righteousness from the greater concentration to the lesser concentration. Ultimately, however, spiritual equilibrium is in fact the goal and purpose of mankind (see Matthew 5:48; 3 Nephi 12:48; 12:27).

If the eternal goal of equilibrium seems to contradict the mortal law of equilibrium, let me give an example. One of the first people I taught on my mission was a university professor who at first appeared very intrigued by the doctrine of mortality, resistance, and what we have referred to as equilibrium, when he read 2 Nephi 2. He taught philosophy, so he sank his mind deeply into such a philosophically enticing scripture. However, after reading the scripture thoroughly, he concluded that our whole existence would be empty if we believed in the necessity of opposition, as taught in 2 Nephi 2. If opposition is necessary, and our goal is to overcome this opposition, he reasoned, then our lives are meaningless. "If your life is spent striving to overcome opposition, what's left to live for once you've met your goal?" he asked us.

At first glance, that is quite a thought. This learned man was basically explaining that an equilibrium universe is in fact a dead universe. So why would we want to achieve this equilibrium by overcoming all opposition? For a short while, it appeared he had a salient point.

But we realized he was missing an understanding of one of the most basic and essential principles of the gospel of Jesus Christ: service. While this man was brilliant, he was missing an understanding of the Father's purpose: to bring to pass the immortality and eternal life of man. We may work to overcome opposition, but we need not worry that we will actually achieve this and be rewarded with nothing but an eternal rocking chair. You see, eternity is not just about us and overcoming our own opposition; it is about all of God's children and helping them all overcome the obstacles of sin and mortality. In fact, the gospel of Jesus Christ teaches us quite clearly that we can't overcome our own opposition unless our lives are spent in the service of our fellow men.

So whatever opposition we may overcome and whatever equilibrium we may ultimately obtain in the eternities, we still have an infinite challenge to help the Father in His goal of bringing to pass the immortality and eternal life of His other children. This is an eternal goal, and the eternities are the only place where we could hope to find the equilibrium that is the goal of nature.

When we understand the Father's purposes and powers and gain our own testimony of service, spiritual equilibrium (following the pattern of physical equilibrium) becomes the most glorious of all eternal goals.

Opposites

The law of opposites is itself another life-sustaining scientific function that also carries spiritual lessons. The same truths that apply to matter at an atomic level apply to life on the human level. Like protons and electrons, men and women are both similar but opposite charges. As protons and electrons are essential components of matter, males and females are both essential components of human life. They are individual creations.

In nature, opposite charges such as protons and electrons attract. It is this attraction that keeps the negatively charged electron in orbit around the nucleus of the atom with its positively charged protons and aptly named neutrons, which have no charge. Without this attraction, atoms, the very building block of all matter, would cease to exist. All life would be over. Without the attraction and union of other opposites, namely man and woman, all life would likewise end. This is the way the Lord has chosen to perpetuate human life. It is not possible in any other way. (Even plants replenish life following a male/female pattern.)

SUMMARY

The symbols inherent in the realm of matter, energy, and science are limited only by our finite understanding of the infinite creations of God. I am no scientist, but it is clear that this is an area of particularly meaningful gospel symbols. We should not shy away from science because it is a secular pursuit. Instead we should treasure it for its divine source. President John Taylor stated: "All the intelligence which men possess on the earth, whether religious, scientific or political—proceeds from God—every good and perfect gift proceeds from Him, the fountain of light and truth, wherein there is no variableness nor shadow of turning. The knowledge of the human system has proceeded from the human system itself, which God has organized."[8]

Elder John A. Widtsoe added:

> Is it any wonder that workers in science, who have been taught the doctrine of an immaterial God who is able to create something from nothing, and to transcend all laws of nature, depart from the faith of their childhood? Truth is truth forever. Scientific truth cannot be theological lie. To the sane mind, theology and philosophy must harmonize. They have the common ground of truth on which to meet.
>
> Thus, on every hand, from the highest to the lowest, from the force of forces and the law of laws to the fundamental laws governing the operations of the universe, and the actions of the individual, the philosophy of the "Mormon" Prophet is consistently referred back to matter, energy and law. In its completeness, it transcends the philosophy of science. Wherever the doctrines of "Mormonism" and science meet, they agree. No discord has yet been found between them. Science is daily confirming the truth of the universe.[9]

The similarities between the gospel of Jesus Christ and science are clear. Science, when properly understood, confirms God; it does not and cannot replace Him.

Notes

1. Albert Einstein, as reported by http://www.quotationspage.com/quote/22864.html.
2. Joseph Smith, Jr., *Teachings of the Prophet Joseph Smith*, comp. Joseph Fielding Smith (Salt Lake City: Deseret Book, 1976), 181.
3. Ibid., 351–52.
4. Ibid., 350–51.
5. *Webster's New World Dictionary, College Edition* (The World Publishing Company, 1962), 491.
6. Ibid., 752.
7. Ibid.
8. Daniel H. Ludlow, *Latter-day Prophets Speak*, first collectors ed. (Salt Lake City: Bookcraft, 1988), 399.
9. John A. Widtsoe, *Joseph Smith as Scientist* (Salt Lake City: Deseret Book, 1908), 147–48; accessed via GospeLink.com.

SECTION TWO

The Law and the Prophets

The Two Great Commandments

The law and the prophets convey divine truths in more ways than one. They teach of the Savior, lead to the Savior, and even embody the Savior.

The Prophet Wilford Woodruff taught,

> The God of heaven, who created this earth and placed His children upon it, gave unto them a law whereby they might be exalted and saved in a kingdom of glory. For there is a law given unto all kingdoms, and all things are governed by law throughout the whole universe. Whatever law anyone keeps he is preserved by that law, and he receives whatever reward that law guarantees unto him. It is the will of God that all His children should obey the highest law, that they may receive the highest glory that is ordained for all immortal beings.[1]

Simply put, the purpose of the law of God is to make us worthy of a celestial glory. If we obey a celestial law, or the law of the Lord, we will inherit a celestial reward, or a reward of God, for "every man receiveth wages of him whom he listeth to obey" (Alma 3:27). Laws or commandments, more than anything else, exist to bring us to Christ. Even physical laws teach us lessons that can help us to be with the Savior eternally and spiritually. If we heed these lessons, we will learn to love God and be closest to Him above any other thing.

The law of God is revealed by His servants, the prophets (see Amos 3:7). For this reason, the "law" is sometimes mentioned together with the "prophets" (see Matthew 7:12; 22:40). In fact, the Old Testament can be viewed largely as the law and the prophets. "If we examine a modern Hebrew Bible and compare the order of its books we shall find that they also fall into three divisions—*The Law, The Prophets, The Writings*."[2] In this sense, the law and the prophets were living prophecies of the Promised Messiah.

Like the law and the prophets, the purpose of the Savior and His Atonement is likewise to make us worthy of a celestial glory. Since the law, the prophets, and the Savior all have the same purpose, and since all things bear witness of and typify Christ, it would logically follow that the law and the prophets would likewise bear witness of Christ and typify Him. There is no question that the law and the prophets teach of Christ, but they also typify Him in ways that we may take for granted. For example, think about the law given to Moses that now serves as the basis (ideally speaking, of course) for civil law on the earth. That law was engraven in stone. As Christ is the rock and the chief cornerstone of our religion (see 1 Peter 2:5–6), the law bears record of Him in this sense. However, there are many more similarities.

The Savior's Great Commandments

Section 76 of the Doctrine and Covenants favors us with one of the greatest visions God has ever revealed to man. This vision was received by Joseph Smith and Sidney Rigdon and contains one of the main doctrines that distinguishes the Church of Jesus Christ of Latter-Day Saints from other denominations. From this revelation we learn that the old sectarian notion limiting the eternities to only a heaven and a hell is false. Christ taught that in His "Father's house are many mansions" (John 14:2; D&C 98:18). In this great vision we learn more about those mansions and about the three degrees in which they are located.

In this vision, the qualifications for attaining these glories are taught and expounded upon. If we view these qualifications broadly, however, we see that the Master had actually revealed these requirements many centuries before. In Matthew we read of these requirements, which have become known as the two great commandments.

> But when the Pharisees had heard that he had put the Sadducees to silence, they were gathered together.
>
> Then one of them, which was a lawyer, asked him a question, tempting him, and saying,

> Master, which is the great commandment in the law?
>
> Jesus said unto him, Thou shalt love the Lord thy God with all thy soul, and with all thy mind.
>
> This is the first and great commandment.
>
> And the second is like unto it, thou shalt love thy neighbour as thyself.
>
> On these two commandments hang all the law and the prophets. (Matthew 22:34–40)

In giving the first great commandment, the Lord gave a summary of the first four commandments of the ten commandments He gave Moses. All of these commandments have to do with God Himself—sanctifying His position as the only God, not taking His name in vain, and keeping His day holy. Placing these commandments first serves as a lesson in priorities. God comes first—period.

The second great commandment, to love our neighbor as ourselves, is the sum of the remaining six commandments received by Moses on Sinai. These command us to respect our parents and the lives, purity, and property of others and not to deceive or covet. With the exception of the fifth commandment, these are commandments of prohibition. For the most part, they direct us what *not* to do. Their placement as the second group of commandments is another lesson in priorities. God comes first, and others are second.

The First Great Commandment and the Celestial Kingdom

Keeping the first commandment could be deemed as putting our Heavenly Father and His eternal will ahead of anything. The Savior's life is the perfect example of this principle (see Luke 22:42). We have the opportunity to fulfill this commandment by covenanting to live the will of the Father rather than our own will and then carrying out that promise.

The first great commandment typifies the law of the celestial kingdom. Those who inherit this glory follow the example of Christ in baptism. They receive, meaning they accept and take into themselves, the testimony of Jesus or the spirit of prophecy (see Revelation 19:10). Because of their faithfulness in keeping the commandments of God, they are cleansed from all sin. Because of their love for God, they are heirs to things that no human eye has seen, nor ear heard, nor heart given welcome to (see 1 Corinthians 2:9). They have completely overcome the Fall and are Christ's even as Christ is God's. They themselves are "gods, even the sons of God" (D&C 76:58). Their love of God surpasses their love of anything else.

The Second Great Commandment and the Terrestrial Kingdom

The second great commandment is to love one's neighbor. It is closely aligned with the first great commandment, and, to be sure, a great many of those who truly keep this commandment have no problem with keeping the first commandment as well. However, those who obey only this commandment do not show the committed love and devotion for their Father in Heaven that would gain them a celestial reward. Therefore, instead of a celestial reward, they receive a lesser reward.

This law typifies the terrestrial kingdom. In the word "terrestrial" we see the Latin "terra," which means earth. This is the kingdom prepared for those who for some reason or another have let the earth or world hinder their devotion to the Lord and His heavenly law.

Recall that Paul taught of these degrees of glory in terms of levels of light. We know that Christ is the "Light of the World" (see D&C 93:9), and science has proven that light travels best through an absence of matter. Likewise, the Savior's light is less inhibited in the absence of matter—"worldly" or "earthly" things—between Him and ourselves. Those who live only this second law may therefore let worldly things inhibit the Light from reaching them.

These are "honorable men of the earth" (D&C 76:75) who "receive of his glory, but not his fulness" (D&C 76:76). Missionaries are tragically aware of such people who do no harm to others and who accept or receive His glory but not His fulness. They may accept the Bible but not the Book of Mormon, even though it is the Book of Mormon that contains the fulness of the gospel of Jesus Christ (see D&C 42:12). These keepers of the terrestrial law but not the celestial law are not valiant in the testimony of Jesus. As the testimony of Jesus is the spirit of prophecy, these people do not quite live "by every word that proceedeth out of the mouth of God" (Matthew 4:4). They gladly live by some of the law and the prophets, but unfortunately not by all of the law and the prophets. While they live honorably, they do not fully embrace the covenants of exaltation that come from living "by every word that proceedeth forth from the mouth of God" (Matthew 4:4).

These are good and honorable people, but their inheritance reflects that they love the things of the earth more than God. They may love their neighbors and live honorably in the world, but it is only unfeigned devotion to God and His commandments that will merit a celestial reward. For this reason, they do not receive a "fulness of the Father" (D&C 76:77).

These people honor their earthly fathers and mothers. They do not kill, commit adultery, steal, bear false witness, or covet their neighbor's property. However, these laws that they gladly keep, are not part of the first great commandment. Keeping the first great commandment consists of more than not killing, not committing adultery, not stealing, not lying, and not coveting. Keeping the first great commandment consists of serving our neighbors, not just refraining from injuring our neighbors. Those who demonstrate love for their neighbors through service are, in effect, serving God (see Mosiah 2:17). True Christianity is found in loving our enemies, blessing those who curse us, doing good to those who hate us, and praying for those who despitefully use us and persecute us (see Matthew 5:44). In other words, loving our neighbors in the truest sense of Christianity extends far beyond the second great commandment.

Living a celestial law is really demonstrated more by what we do than what we don't do. It would be foolish to believe that we could inherit the celestial kingdom merely by not murdering, stealing, committing adultery, and so forth. To receive a celestial glory, it is not enough just to empty our lives of seriously sinful behavior; we must also fill our lives with good, with service and kindness to our neighbors and devotion to God. This kind of behavior is truly what it means to keep the first great commandment (see Matthew 25:40).

The Third Commandment and the Telestial Kingdom

Finally, in the telestial kingdom, we see not the first or second great commandment, but the "third commandment" that so many people live. It is not loving God, or loving one's neighbor, but loving oneself. The heirs of the telestial kingdom are described as being "as innumerable as the stars in the firmament of heaven, or as the sand upon the seashore" (D&C 76:109). This vast number is probably roughly equal to those all around us in the world who, like Lucifer, would list their favorite words as "I," "me," "my," and "mine," (see Moses 4:1–4). This is a stark contrast to the Savior, whose hallmark words were, "nevertheless not my will, but thine, be done" (Luke 22:42).

These are the same people who seek not the will of God nor receive the gospel of Christ (see D&C 76:81–89). These are the ones who fall prey to pride and choose their own will over the will of God. In fact, a good definition of pride might be misguided love. It is not love for God, or for one's neighbor, but for oneself. Since the natural man is an enemy to God (see Mosiah 3:19), this is not a good place for one's wholehearted devotion.

There is nothing wrong with loving yourself. However, there is great danger in loving yourself more than your neighbor and more than your Creator. Ironically, like so many principles in the gospel, loving God first makes it so much easier to show love for a neighbor and, in a healthy way, love for yourself. In fact, this is the only way to true happiness.

Some of the best counsel I have ever received reflects this wisdom and the frustration that comes from living the "third great commandment" and not the first and second. I was once told, "The next time you're feeling down, look around yourself, and I will bet you anything you will be thinking of yourself." How true that counsel has proven through the years. Since I received that counsel, I have consistently noticed that my times of sorrow have so often come from self-pity when I was wallowing in the "third great commandment" and thinking only of myself.

By contrast, my "mission mother," Diana Bird Holt, the wife of my second mission president, R. Douglas Holt, lived an unforgettable example of selflessness. She was gravely injured in a car accident as a teenager and lived the rest of her life in constant pain from those injuries. She underwent multiple surgeries—literally dozens of them—over the next twenty-five years or so to try to correct this condition, but the only relief she found was temporary at best.

When her injuries finally claimed her life only a few years after her mission call, I will never forget the words spoken by her husband at her funeral. You see, she coped with her pain by serving—by volunteering at hospitals and serving any way she could. "When the pain got so great," recalled President Holt, "she would pray, 'Heavenly Father, please send someone to help.' "

Now, this prayer is probably quite common, but she offered it in a completely different way from the rest of the world. Unlike most who would utter such a prayer, she was not pleading for the Lord to send someone to help *her*; she was pleading for the Lord to send someone *she* could help. Her joy and her relief were found in ministering to others, in living the first great commandment when so many in her position would have searched for that joy and relief by thinking of themselves. What a wonderful model of the Savior's love!

It is so ironic, yet appropriate, that truly keeping the first great commandment takes care of all the other commandments as well. Truly, this kind of service is what the Lord meant when He said, "He who seeketh to save his life shall lose it: and he that loseth his life for my sake shall find it" (JST Matthew 10:34; see also Matthew 10:39).[3]

Christ as the Fulfillment of the Law and the Prophets

How do these great commandments bear witness of the Lord? Christ is found within the law itself. "If any man will do his will [i.e., follow the law and keep the commandments], he shall know of the doctrine, whether it be of God, or whether I speak of myself" (John 7:17).

Christ Himself personified the law. He was the perfect example of loving God. His sacrifice was the ultimate representation of loving one's neighbor as well as the Father. Quite simply, keeping the Lord's law makes us more like Him. In fact, the law of God is nothing more or less than a definition and description of the Master's life. That life is the perfect example of how we should love our Heavenly Father and our neighbors.

The law is also fulfilled in Him. Note the concluding statement of the Savior's lesson on the two great commandments. He states, on these two great commandments "hang all the law and the prophets" (Matthew 22:40). This same phrase appears nine other times in the scriptures, so it must obviously have some great significance.[4] The entire purpose of all prophets and commandments is to bring us unto Christ (see Galatians 3:24; Mosiah 16:14–15; Helaman 8:14–20). As the phrase "the law and the prophets" especially describes the Old Testament, the law and the prophets proceeding Christ specifically served to prepare the people for Him.

Consider again the chiastic pattern of the earth's history and the Old and New Testaments.

OLD TESTAMENT (COVENANT)
    ADVENT OF CHRIST
NEW TESTAMENT (COVENANT)

Again we can see that the Lord's birth divides the Old and New Testaments. The center or focal point is Christ Himself. The Old Testaments, here described as "the law and the prophets," lead directly to Christ, both physically and spiritually.

Now notice again that on "these two commandments hang all the law and the prophets" (Matthew 22:40). For a law to "hang on" or gain its support from something, that something must be greater than the law itself. The law and the prophets led the people to Christ so that He could give them a greater law and so that the law could be fulfilled in Him (see Matthew 5:17; 3 Nephi 12:17). With the coming of Christ, the higher law of Christianity was personified.

While the law and the prophets taught people not to commit adultery, kill, or steal, the greater law announced by Christ teaches us not even to look on a woman to lust (see Matthew 5:28; 3 Nephi 12:28); it teaches us to love our enemies, bless those who curse us, do good to those that hate us, and pray for those who despitefully use us and persecute us (see Matthew 5:44; 3 Nephi 12:44). In Christ's law the negative prohibitions are replaced with positive admonitions. The essence of true Christianity is found in the fulfillment of the law and the prophets. "And for this cause he is the mediator of the new covenant, that by means of death, for the redemption of the transgressions that were under the first covenant, they which are called might receive the promise of eternal inheritance" (JST Hebrews 9:15).

The highest law and covenant correspond with the highest glory. Both the highest law and highest glory belong to the Lord. Seeking and loving the Lord first is the focus of the law, and it paves the way for all other rewards that come from obedience to the law (see Matthew 6:33; Luke 12:31; 3 Nephi 13:33; D&C 11:23). Since it is the purpose of the law and the prophets to bring us to Christ, we will become His if we keep the first great commandment. And to become His is to become God's (see D&C 76:59).

Christ as the Source of the Law

The law also symbolizes Christ in that He is the One who gave it. Far too many good Christian people do not understand that Christ is Jehovah, the God of the Old Testament, who gave the law to Moses. This simple, beautiful lesson is taught plainly in the Book of Mormon by the Savior Himself.

> And it came to pass that when Jesus had said these words he perceived that there were some among them who marveled, and wondered what he would concerning the law of Moses; for they understood not the saying that old things had passed away, and that all things had become new.
>
> And he said unto them: Marvel not that I said unto you that old things had passed away, and that all things had become new.
>
> Behold I say unto you that the law is fulfilled that was given unto Moses.
>
> *Behold, I am he that gave the law,* and I am he who covenanted with my people Israel; therefore, the law in me is fulfilled, for I have come to fulfil the law; therefore it hath an end.
>
> Behold, I do not destroy the prophets, for as many as have not been fulfilled in me, verily I say unto you, shall all be fulfilled. (3 Nephi 15:2–6; emphasis added)

The Doctrine and Covenants also teaches that Jesus Christ is and was Jehovah. "Wherefore, hear my voice and follow me, and you shall be a free people, and ye shall have no laws but my laws when I come, for I am your lawgiver" (D&C 38:22).

Likewise, Section 110 teaches:

> We saw the Lord standing upon the breastwork of the pulpit, before us; and under his feet was a paved work of pure gold, in color like amber.
>
> His eyes were as a flame of fire; the hair of his head was white like the pure snow; his countenance shone above the brightness of the sun; and his voice was as the sound of the rushing of great waters, even the voice of Jehovah, saying:
>
> I am the first and the last; I am he who liveth, I am he who was slain; I am your advocate with the Father. (D&C 110:2–4)

Christ is the very author of the law, as it was given in the Old Testament, the New Testament, and as it is still being revealed in latter days.

He is the Jehovah of the Old Testament, and the Old Testament law was a very literal prophecy of Him. When He was born in Bethlehem, He personified and fulfilled that law.

He truly is both the beginning and ending, the Alpha and Omega, referring to the first and last letters of the Greek alphabet (see Revelation 1:8, 11; 22:13). He is also called the First and the Last (see Isaiah 41:4; 44:6; 48:12). He is the beginning, or the First, because He gave the law. He is the end, or the Last, because the law met its fulfillment in Him. And as He is both the beginning and ending, it only makes sense that Christ is also the center of that law and that He is depicted in the rites and ordinances of the law. As He said, "Behold, I am the law and the light. Look unto me, and endure to the end, and ye shall live; for unto him that endureth to the end will I give eternal life" (3 Nephi 15:9).

Notes

1. Wilford Woodruff, *The Discourses of Wilford Woodruff*, comp. G. Homer Durham (Salt Lake City: Bookcraft, 1990), 10.
2. Sidney B. Sperry, *Spirit of the Old Testament* (Salt Lake City: Deseret Book, 1940), 2; accessed via GospeLink.com.
3. This scripture appears so important that the Lord actually repeated it during His ministry as accounted in the gospels. It is actually found five different times in the gospels and in the Joseph Smith Translation (Matthew 16:25; Mark 8:35; Luke 9:24; Luke 17:33).
4. See Matthew 7:12; Luke 16:16; John 1:45; Acts 13:15; Acts 24:14; Romans 3:21; 3 Nephi 14:12; 3 Nephi 15:10; D&C 59:22.

The Old Testament Law of Sacrifice

The sacrificial rites of the Old Testament law were a striking typification of Christ. As Abinadi preached:

> And now I say unto you that it was expedient that there should be a law given to the children of Israel, yea, even a very strict law; for they were a stiffnecked people, quick to do iniquity, and slow to remember the Lord their God;
>
> Therefore there was a law given them, yea, a law of performances and of ordinances, a law which they were to observe strictly from day to day, to keep them in remembrance of God and their duty towards him.
>
> But behold, I say unto you, that all these things were types of things to come. (Mosiah 13:29–31)

Animal Sacrifice

It's not completely accurate to associate animal sacrifice with only the Mosaic law. Animal sacrifice was actually instituted after the Fall to teach Adam and Eve of the Savior who would come and atone for the sins of the world.

> And after many days an angel of the Lord appeared unto Adam, saying: Why dost thou offer sacrifices unto the Lord? And Adam said unto him: I know not, save the Lord commanded me.
>
> And then the angel spake, saying: This thing is a similitude of the sacrifice of the Only Begotten of the Father, which is full of grace and truth.

> Wherefore, thou shalt do all that thou doest in the name of the Son, and thou shalt repent and call upon God in the name of the Son forevermore. (Moses 5:6–8)

Cain and Abel were both commanded to offer sacrifices long before the time of Moses (see Genesis 4:3–4). Noah offered sacrifices after the flood (see Genesis 8:20). Likewise, Abraham and his posterity clearly understood the commandments and lessons of sacrifices many years before Moses (see Genesis 22).

Therefore, while animal sacrifices were certainly a part of the law of Moses, the principle is not unique to the Mosaic law. As the LDS Bible Dictionary teaches, "Whenever there were true believers on the earth, with priesthood authority, sacrifices were offered in that manner and for that purpose. This continued until the death of Jesus Christ, which ended the shedding of blood as a gospel ordinance."

Still, some the most instructive lessons on animal sacrifice come specifically from the Mosaic law. Those sacrifices clearly foreshadowed the Messiah and taught of Him. The sacrifices also served as the center of religious services, much like sacrament meeting or a temple endowment session does in our day (see Genesis 4:3–7; 8:20; 22:1–17; Exodus 5:3; 20:24; Job 1:5; 42:8). And just like with temple service and sacrament meetings, it is more important to focus on the symbolic message of the sacrifice than its ceremonial aspects. Furthermore, understanding the symbolism conveyed in the sacrifice should lead to a deeper appreciation of the ceremonies that are centered on it.

In every sacrificial offering, there were "at least three distinct objects presented. . . . There is the offering, the priest, the offerer."[1] Of these three, the sacrificial animal is the most obvious representation of Christ; however, as we will see, all three of these objects—not just the offering—represent Christ.

The Offering

The Bible records many different kinds of animals to be offered as sacrifices. After a reprieve from the commandment to offer his son, Abraham offered a ram (see Genesis 22:13). Moses was commanded to offer two lambs at the tabernacle, one in the morning and one in the evening (see Exodus 29:38–42). The same sacrifice of two lambs—one in the morning and one in the evening—was later commanded as an offering every Sabbath (see Numbers 28:4, 9–10). At the beginning of each month, two young bullocks, one ram, and seven unblemished lambs in their first year were to be offered (see Numbers 28:11). Goats, sometimes young ones, were particular "sin" offerings (see Numbers 28:15, 22, 30).

The Lamb

Of all the animals ever offered, the most familiar and fitting sacrificial animal was a male lamb without blemish—the firstborn of the flock to be sacrificed without breaking a bone (see Genesis 4:4; Exodus 12:5; Leviticus 14:10; Leviticus 23:12; Numbers 9:12). This is one of the most obvious types of the Lamb of God, who is Christ (see John 1:29).

In six ways the sacrificial lamb was a type for Jesus Christ:

1. No bones of the lamb were to be broken (see Psalms 34:20; Exodus 12:46; John 19:36).
2. The lamb was to be perfect (see Malachi 1:7–14; 3 Nephi 12:48).
3. The lamb was to be without blemish (see Exodus 12:5; Hebrews 7:26–27; 1 Peter 2:22).
4. The flesh of the lamb was to be eaten (see Exodus 12:8; John 6:53–55).
5. The lamb had to be the firstborn (see Exodus 13:2; D&C 93:21).
6. The lamb had to be male (see Exodus 12:5; Matthew 1:21).

The early Christians knew that just as the blood of the lamb had saved the ancient Israelites from temporal death during the first Passover, even so would Christ, "our passover" (1 Corinthians 5:7), save those of righteous Israel from spiritual death (Hebrews 9:20–22).[2]

Just like the sacrificial lamb, Christ was the Firstborn of God (see D&C 93:21; Luke 2:6–7). He was sacrificed in the cruelest manner imaginable, yet not a bone of His body was broken (see John 19:36). He was the perfect one, without blemish (see 1 Peter 2:22). Symbolically speaking, we eat His flesh with the sacrament (see Matthew 26:26). Who could believe this was all a coincidence? Further, of all the titles applied to Christ in the scriptures, "the Lamb" is one of the most prevalent.[3]

Why a Lamb?

For one, lambs are known as particularly gentle, loveable, and obedient animals. While fiercer animals such as a lion are accurately used to represent the Savior's power (see Genesis 49:8–12; Revelation 5:5), it is the more gentle and loving qualities of the Savior that are most appropriately revealed and repeated above all others. The title of the Lamb places particular emphasis on the fact that He is meek and lowly of heart (see Matthew 11:29). To us, this is a lesson that He is perfectly approachable and welcoming to the penitent.

These qualities demonstrate the Savior's constant invitation to come unto Him, the gentle healer. "Behold, doth he cry unto any, saying: Depart from me? Behold, I say unto you, Nay; but he saith: Come unto me all ye ends of the earth, buy milk and honey, without money and without price" (2 Nephi 26:25; see also 2 Nephi 9:50).

The Savior's title as the Lamb also illustrates His qualities of obedience and innocence as our perfect example. We are taught that we should come unto Christ by becoming as innocent and docile as a little child (see 3 Nephi 11:37, 38; Mark 10:15; Luke 18:17). A lamb is a young sheep—a "little child" among sheep—and sheep are known for their penchant to hear and follow their leaders obediently (see John 10:27). A lamb is therefore a unique combination of obedience and innocence. These are the exact qualities that we are invited to emulate in following the example of the Savior. In our quest to apply the Atonement to our own lives, we are taught to become as a little child, even as the Lamb.

Christ is also the Good Shepherd, who cares for His own lambs (see Psalms 23:1; John 10:14). As we become like the Lamb of God, we join the flock of the Good Shepherd. We listen for and obey His voice (see Alma 5:57). All the lambs in the flock are invited to follow Him, and He calls His lambs by His own name (see Alma 5:38).

In summary, the Lamb is the personification of mercy, the epitome of obedience, approachability, and loveable innocence. "And now, the plan of mercy could not be brought about except an atonement should be made; therefore God himself atoneth for the sins of the world, to bring about the plan of mercy, to appease the demands of justice, that God might be a perfect, just God and a merciful God also" (Alma 42:15). The price for us to meet the demands of justice and also have access to mercy was the ultimate Sacrificial Lamb.

The Priest

It was the role of a priest like Aaron to slay the sacrificial animal and thus make the offering. "For every high priest taken from among men is ordained for men in things pertaining to God, that he may offer both gifts and sacrifices for sins. . . . And no man taketh this honour unto himself, but he that was called of God, as was Aaron" (Hebrews 5:1, 4).

The Priest as a Representative

The priest's role, both anciently and in modern times, might be summarized as making the blessings of the sacrifice available to the people. The priest was an important intermediary between the people and the Lord, since the priest made the offering on behalf of the people (see Leviticus 4:20). Following a similar pattern, a priest still blesses and administers the sacrament in our sacrament meetings today on behalf of the congregation.

Likewise, a priest in the Aaronic Priesthood today shares some of the ministerial duties in the restored gospel including preaching, teaching, expounding, exhorting, and baptizing (see D&C 20:46–47). In ancient times, the people literally looked to the priest to make this offering on their behalf, and the pattern continues today, even if we might not think of a sixteen-year-old boy as the perfect type of Christ.

The Priest and the Blood of the Sacrifice

In addition to offering the sacrifice, the priest was under a particular duty to care for the blood of the animal.

> When the Lord gave Israel their system of animal sacrifices, all to be performed in similitude of the future sacrifice of their Messiah, he singled out the blood as the sacrificial element to which special attention should be given. It was not the flesh of the sacrificial animal, not the sacred altar on which the Lord's fires burned, not the manner in which the Levites should perform their ministerial labors (though all these had a bearing and bore a relative share of importance), but it was the blood of the animals that concerned the Lord. He gave, as we have seen, detailed instructions as to sprinkling the blood in the ransoming rituals, and the blood was singled out as the symbol of the whole atoning process.
>
> Indeed, so sacred was the blood element in the sacrificial ordinance

> that Jehovah directed Moses to forbid the people to eat any blood at any time, lest they fail to reverence, as his law required, the particular blood chosen to make an atonement for them. The penalty for disobedience to what otherwise would have been an irrelevant and unreasonable dietary restriction was to be severed from one's inheritance in Israel. The penalty for any soul who ate blood was to be "cut off from among his people." . . .
>
> With all this in mind, no longer need men ask, "Why this emphasis on the shedding of blood? Why dwell with such emphasis, and so repetitively on our Lord's death and the manner in which it came to pass?" The reasons are clear and compelling. Where salvation is concerned, we are dealing with life and death; we are born into mortality so that we may have the privilege of dying and coming forth in immortality. In our search for salvation, we are dealing with mortal life and mortal death; we are dealing with immortality and eternal life; we are seeking to learn how mortality becomes immortality, and how men, having bowed to the natural death, can yet come forth and gain eternal life. To crystallize in our minds and to dramatize before our eyes what is involved in all this, the Lord has chosen blood as the symbol of both life and death.[4]

It was the priest who tore the flesh of the sacrifice so that the blood would spill. This is also modeled in the restored gospel. The priest tears the bread, which represents the body of Christ. This torn flesh leads to the pouring out of His blood, represented by the second part of the ordinance—the water. While spilling the blood of an innocent lamb is undeniably more drastic and poignant than the bread and water we now use, the symbolism is the same, and therefore the message and its importance are the same.

As noted previously, the dramatic symbolism of spilling an innocent animal's blood was designed to affix firmly in everyone's mind and heart the fact that the Messiah and His sacrifice are quite literally a matter of life and death. This is the nature of eternity. We are dealing with men's souls. The stakes could not be higher, and animal sacrifices where life somehow came through death were designed specifically to pound that lesson deep within us.

The High Priest on the Day of Atonement

One particular priest held a specific duty in the temple of not just slaying animals, but of performing the most sacred rite in Israel. Each year the Jews celebrated their most holy day, the Day of Atonement, which is still revered by the Jews as Yom Kippur. This was a sort of Sabbath among Sabbaths and the only day when all of Israel fasted.[5] On that day, the high priest parted the veil of the temple and entered the most sacred place in the tabernacle, known as the Holy of Holies (see Hebrews 9:7, 12).

When he entered, he took with him the blood of the special sacrifices offered that day. He sprinkled this blood on and before the mercy seat, which symbolized the actual presence of God (see Leviticus 16:14–15; Exodus 25:22). Interestingly, "mercy seat" may also be properly translated as "atonement cover" (Exodus 25:17, see footnote a). This name illustrates the effect that the Atonement has of "covering" our sins before the Lord. "Blessed is he whose transgression is forgiven, whose sin is covered . . . unto whom the Lord imputeth not iniquity" (Psalms 32:1, 2). "To cover" is in fact one of the definitions of the Hebrew word for atonement.[6]

In this context, the high priest didn't just shed or collect the blood; he brought it to the Holy of Holies—the symbolic presence of God—to atone for the sins of Israel and to cover their sins before God. While the priest shed the blood on the altar in the outer court of the Tabernacle, it might be said that the high priest applied the blood on this holiest of occasions and in the holiest of places in all of Israel.

In symbolically entering the presence of God and offering this blood, the high priest was carrying the load of all of Israel's sins and taking the people back into the presence of the Lord. This was the only day and, therefore, the only appropriate opportunity in the symbolic presence of God for the sacred name of Jehovah to be spoken. Obviously, the high priest carried a tremendous duty to be worthy to carry the most important sacrificial blood into the most holy place and utter the most holy name. He was the only one who could do so, and even then it was only at the most holy and divinely appointed time.

The Symbolism of the Priest

Who, then, is symbolized by the priest, who spilled the sacrificial blood on behalf of the people? And who is symbolized by the high priest who parted the veil and entered the presence of Deity, bearing the choicest blood and uttering the most holy name?

In both instances, it is Christ. The book of Hebrews, which Paul wrote to teach the Hebrews of the meaning behind the rites and ordinances they had been practicing for generations, makes many references to Christ as the Priest or High Priest. "Wherefore, holy brethren, partakers of the heavenly calling, consider the Apostle and High Priest of our profession, Christ Jesus" (Hebrews 3:1; see also Hebrews 4:14; 7:26; 8:1; 9:11).

Consider the similarities:

- Like the priest offering the sacrifice, the Savior alone had the power to allow His own blood to be spilled and His own life to be taken (see 1 Nephi 19:9–10).
- Like the high priest entering the Holy of Holies in the temple, Christ alone had the power to enter the presence of the Father because of the perfect life He lived. "Having therefore, brethren, boldness to enter the holiest by the blood of Jesus, By a new and living way, which he hath consecrated for us, through the veil, that is to say, his flesh; And having an high priest over the house of God" (Hebrews 10:19–21; see also Hebrews 6:19–20).
- Finally, like the high priest, Jesus alone had the power to apply this blood and offer the Atonement for all those who would obey the laws and ordinances of His gospel (see Alma 22:14).

This rich symbolism reminds us even more deeply of the Savior's majesty. Not only was His sacrifice essential to eternity, but He was the only one qualified to make that sacrifice because of the perfect life He had lived. This is also a great lesson to holders of His priesthood. Your duty as holders of that same priesthood is to make the Atonement available to the saints, as did the priest and high priest anciently. This should be the focus of every priesthood action performed. This duty is not to be taken lightly. It is based on the precise example of the Savior Himself.

The Offerer

In ancient sacrifices, the offerer would be the owner of the sacrificial animal to be offered. He would present the sacrifice as his own contribution, his own property.

The sacrificial animal would then have hands laid on its head to dedicate it as a proxy or substitute for another's sins (see Leviticus 16:21).[7] This act of laying on hands represented the transfer of guilt and sin to the animal. This is an obvious reference to the Messiah, the Anointed One who bears guilt for our sins vicariously; He does for us what we cannot do for ourselves.

Who, then, is represented by the offerer? Again, the offerer is a symbol of Christ because He freely presented Himself as the sacrifice (see Galatians 1:4). His life was His alone to present. As we sing, "His life he freely gave, A sinless sacrifice for guilt, A dying world to save."[8] In a way that we cannot understand in mortality, the debt of our sins was transferred to Him of His own free will and choice. And in similitude of the sacrifice offered by Christ, we too are invited to offer our hearts (see 3 Nephi 9:19–20) and souls (see Omni 1:26) so that we can receive the benefits of the Savior's sacrifice.

The Sacrifice, the Priest, and the Offerer All as Christ

> What, then, is the offering? what is the priest? what is the offerer? Christ is the offering, Christ is the priest, Christ is the offerer. Such and so manifold are the relations in which Christ has stood for man and to man, that no one type or set of types can adequately represent the fulness of them . . . As man under the law, our substitute, Christ stood for us towards God as offerer . . . thus His body was His offering: He willingly offered it; and as the priest he took the blood into the holiest. As offerer, we see Him man under the law, standing our substitute, for us to fulfil all righteousness. As priest, we have Him presented as the mediator, God's messenger between Himself and Israel. While as the offering He is seen the innocent victim, a sweet savour to God, yet bearing the sin dying for it.[9]

Here is symbolism at its most compelling. We may have a limited or even an appreciable understanding of the Savior as the sacrifice, but we are still really only scratching the surface of a true appreciation of the Savior. In seeing Him not just as the sacrifice but also as the offerer of that sacrifice, the priest administering that sacrifice, and the high priest applying that sacrifice before the Father, we see so much more of just how magnificent and incomparable our Savior truly is. No one else could perform any of the indispensable roles of the Atonement, much less all of them.

The Blessings of the Atonement Reflected in the Sacrifices

There were four kinds of Old Testament sacrifices that specifically foreshadowed the Savior's Atonement. These sacrifices were sin offerings, trespass or guilt offerings, peace offerings, and burnt offerings. These separate and distinct offerings are each lessons in the Atonement in that they teach of the effects of the Atonement on the repentant soul. In other words, these sacrifices teach of the different types of shortcomings we experience in mortality that can be overcome through the Atonement. At the same time, they also teach of the effect that the Atonement is designed to have on us.

Sin Offerings

As is clear from the name, these offerings were meant to atone for Israel's sins. This category included both unintentional acts (see Leviticus 4) and certain intentional acts or crimes (see Leviticus 6). These offerings represent the outright sins—the knowing and conscious acts we commit against the will of God—that the Atonement serves to cover.

Trespass or Guilt Offerings

These offerings applied to sins that caused injury to someone. These were not specifically sins against God but trespasses against a neighbor. In our imperfect modern-day legal system, we might look to the courts to redress a loss or a heartbreak from something like a car accident caused by a careless driver. Under the Mosaic law, however, the wrongdoer looked to God for forgiveness as well as redress. The trespass or guilt offering was the medium for that forgiveness (see Leviticus 5). This is another function of the Atonement. It makes up not just for outright sins, but for any other trespasses—all the losses, griefs, and sorrows that man can endure (see Isaiah 53:4–5; Alma 7:11).

Burnt Offerings

In burnt offerings, the entire animal was burned (see Leviticus 1:9). The smoke of the offering ascended to heaven throughout the day. This is meant to teach two specific symbolic lessons of the Atonement. First, the complete consumption of the sacrifice is a lesson about the effect that the Atonement is meant to have on us. It is meant to consume us to the core and burn away the old creature—the natural man—entirely (see Mosiah 3:19). When we offer our "whole souls as an offering unto him," we follow the lesson taught by the symbolism of a burnt offering (see Omni 1:26).

Second, the continual smoke from this complete sacrifice is a representation of prayer. Much like the incense that burned before the veil in the temple, this is a reminder that prayer is an essential principle that gives us access to the Atonement.[10] For example, when Adam was taught the symbolism behind the sacrifices he offered, he was also instructed to call upon the Lord in prayer in the name of the Son forevermore (see Moses 5:5–8). In other words, he was instructed to pray unceasingly in connection with his sacrifice. Prayer and sacrifice are inseparably connected, as illustrated by burnt offerings.

Peace Offerings

As you would expect, this symbolizes the blessing of peace that comes through the Atonement. The Savior is the Prince of Peace (see Isaiah 9:6), so this offering was a lesson about the peace that awaits the penitent, those who apply the Savior's atoning blood by obedience to the laws and ordinances of the gospel.

Summary

Can you imagine how a priest in Old Testament times must have felt when offering a sacrifice on behalf of his people? The priest was representing the Lord Himself in an action so startling and compelling that it was the only thing that could illustrate the necessity of the Atonement and the absolute life and death issue that was at stake. Likewise, can you imagine being the high priest in the tabernacle and temple, symbolically entering the presence of God—the holiest place on earth—to offer the atoning blood for your fellow Israelites? How humbling it must have been to stand in the place of the Lord and prefigure His Atonement in such a compelling manner! What a lesson for the priests and high priests in the Lord's restored Church to learn and follow today!

If we miss the point of this striking symbolism, we have completely missed the point of one of the deepest lessons on the Atonement that the Lord has given us. Even though we are no longer required to offer innocent animals, we would do well to learn from the Old Testament symbols that so poignantly illustrate the drama and lessons of the Atonement. Only gospel symbolism can truly convey these lessons to the human mind and embed them in the human heart.

Notes

1. Andrew Jukes, *The Law of the Offerings: The Five Tabernacle Offerings and Their Spiritual Significance* (Grand Rapids, MI: Kregel Classics, 2004), 44–45.
2. McConkie & Parry, *A Guide to Scriptural Symbols*, 141–42.
3. See Isaiah 53:7; John 1:29; 1 Peter 1:19; Revelation 5:6, 12; 7:14; 12:11; 13:8; 14:1; 17:14; 19:7; 19:9; 21:23; 22:3; 1 Nephi 10:10; 11:21; 12:11; 13:40; 41:1; Mosiah 14:7; Alma 7:14; 13:11; Helaman 6:5; Mormon 9:6; Ether 13:11; D&C 58:11; 65:3; 76:21, 39, 85, 119; 88:106; 109:79; 133:56; Moses 7:47.
   It is interesting to note that the title "Lamb" was a particular favorite of John, "the disciple whom Jesus loved" (John 13:23; 19:26; 20:2; 21:7, 20). This is evidenced by the frequent use of the term in the book of Revelation.
4. Bruce R. McConkie, *The Promised Messiah* (Salt Lake City: Deseret Book, 1990), 257–259.
5. *Smith's Bible Dictionary*, 28.
6. Strong, *Strong's Exhaustive Concordance of the Bible,* Hebrew word 3722.
7. In many cases, the offerer also took on the role of the priest by slaying the animal.
8. *Hymns*, no. 195.
9. Jukes, *The Law of Offerings*, 44–45.
10. McConkie & Parry, *A Guide to Scriptural Symbols*, 68–69.

The Mosaic Law Feasts

Under the Mosaic law, there were three major "feasts" each year. These feasts corresponded with great events in Hebrew history and days that were held as sacred. To celebrate these feasts, the men were required to gather and symbolically appear before the Lord around the temple in Jerusalem to renew their covenants. This is the same practice seen in the Book of Mormon when King Benjamin gathered his people together to hear his words of counsel. By no coincidence, King Benjamin's people were also gathered to observe the sacrifices and offerings of the Mosaic law (see Mosiah 2:1–4).

While there were other feasts, the feasts of the Passover, Pentecost, and Tabernacles were the major feasts that all men were actually required to attend and celebrate by offering their worship and devotion to the Lord. These feasts were specially appointed times for the Israelites to express their gratitude and remember certain events when the hand of the Lord had been plainly revealed to their forefathers. In this attitude of remembrance, the Israelites were prepared to draw nearer to their God, just as we are invited to do each week when we partake of the sacrament in remembrance of the Atonement. Each of these feasts is a direct representation of the Savior in its subject matter and form of celebration.

The Feast of Passover: Origins of the Passover

For generations, the Israelites were slaves to Egypt. This period of slavery was foretold through Abraham, who was told "thy seed shall be a stranger in a land that is not theirs, and shall serve them; and they shall afflict them four hundred years" (Genesis 15:13). This prophecy was fulfilled at the beginning of the book of Exodus, where we read, "Therefore they did set over them taskmasters to afflict them with their burdens" (Exodus 1:11). This period of slavery continued for an overwhelming 430 years (see Exodus 12:40–41).

Toward the end of this period of slavery, the Lord sent a series of plagues to Egypt in an effort to compel the release of the Israelites so that they might serve God (see Exodus 8:1; 9:1; 10:3). These plagues included a flooding of frogs that filled the land and then died (see Exodus 8:2–14); a mass infestation of lice (see Exodus 8:16–18); swarms of flies (see Exodus 8:21–32); the loss of all the cattle in Egypt (see Exodus 9:3–7); a plague of boils and blains, or swelling sores (see Exodus 9:9–11); and, literally, a hail of fire (see Exodus 9:18–34). The last plague was almost enough to persuade Pharaoh to let the Israelites go, but Moses perceived that Pharaoh was insincere in his repentance, and the hail of fire continued (see Exodus 9:27–35).

Then more plagues followed, this time with waves of locusts to fill everything that hadn't already been destroyed (see Exodus 10:4–6, 12–15). Like before, Pharaoh showed a hint of penitence, but it was insincere and predictably short-lived (see JST Exodus 10:16–20).

Because of Pharaoh's continuing hard-heartedness, the Lord then sent a plague of thick darkness that lasted three days (see Exodus 10:21–23), just like what the Nephites endured when Christ was crucified and the Light of the World was taken from the world (see 3 Nephi 8:20–23). Pharaoh responded to this plague by telling Moses to leave and that he would kill Moses the next time they saw each other (see Exodus 10:28). However, the Joseph Smith Translation of this section clarifies that Pharaoh yet again hardened his heart and would not relent.

Finally, Moses told the Egyptians that the last plague the Lord had decreed was the death of every firstborn in Egypt, including Pharaoh's own son, the heir to the throne (see Exodus 11:5). In order to avoid this most horrible of all plagues, Moses instructed each Israelite family to slaughter a male lamb without blemish, striking the lamb's blood on their door posts (see Exodus 12:3–7). Those who followed these instructions and applied the blood of the lamb to their homes were spared the terror of this plague. Those who did not lost their firstborn (see Exodus 12:29). For Pharaoh, the loss of his firstborn son was finally enough to convince him to let the Israelites leave with all of their flocks and herds (see Exodus 12:31, 32).

After more than four hundred years of captivity, it was cause for an entire nation to celebrate. Their celebration took the form of Passover (see Exodus 12:14–28).

Symbolism of the Passover

To understand the symbolism in this story, it is first important to understand that Egypt represents the world or "that which is forbidden" (Abraham 1:23). As a scriptural symbol, Egypt isn't quite as blatantly evil as Babylon, but it clearly represents the things of the world that tend to hold us captive, whatever those things may be. In other words, each of us has our own Egypt, or Egypts, to escape.

The Israelites represent the true believers in the Lord.[1] Just as Egypt enslaved ancient Israel for over four hundred years, the things of the world (e.g., riches, luxury, fame, keeping up with the Joneses) tend to enslave modern Israel—members of the Lord's restored Church—today. Moses is an obvious symbol for the Savior. He led the covenant people out of bondage, just as the Savior leads us out of spiritual bondage. He alone is mighty enough to humble and defeat the Pharaohs of today's world.

Central to the Passover is another symbol of Christ, one which led to the liberation of Israel—the blood of the Lamb. Sprinkling the blood of the Passover lamb on their doorposts reminded the Israelites of the destroying angel passing over their forefathers and allowing them to escape the snares of Egypt. "And the blood shall be to you for a token upon the houses where ye are: and when I see the blood, I will pass over you, and the plague shall not be upon you to destroy you when I smite the land of Egypt" (Exodus 12:13).

This was an unmistakable type of "the blood of Christ, which should fall as drops in Gethsemane and flow in a stream from a pierced side as he hung on the cross, and would cleanse and save the faithful; and that those in Israel were saved temporally because the blood of a sacrificial lamb was sprinkled on the doorposts of their houses, so the faithful of all ages would wash their garments in the blood of the Eternal Lamb and from him receive an eternal salvation."[2] The firstborn of Egypt died, symbolizing the death of those worldly things that ensnare us; while the Firstborn of God brought eternal life to all those who applied His blood.

This may also be a lesson on the importance of families and the home. It was the families who either suffered or were spared from the destroying angel. It was at the home, or more specifically the entry to the home, that the token of the Lamb's blood was either rightly applied or missing. The life or death of the family literally depended on the family members blessing their homes with the symbolic token of the Atonement. Today, spiritual life or death is likewise determined within the walls of the home. The battle with the destroying angel is fought not in some distant ancient land but right in our own homes. As always the key to spiritual survival is applying the atoning blood of the Lamb on our symbolic doorposts, that our incomings and "outgoings may be in the name of the Lord" (D&C 88:120).

In further symbolism of the Atonement, the Passover lamb was to be sacrificed without breaking a bone (see Exodus 12:46). As taught by John, when the Savior was mercilessly sacrificed, not a bone of His body was broken (see John 19:36).

In commemorating the first Passover, the later Israelites celebrated seven days of feasting known as the Feast of Unleavened Bread (see Exodus 12:15, 17). The unleavened bread symbolized the haste with which the Israelites left their captivity when they had the chance. They didn't even wait for their bread to rise, figuratively speaking. This represents the urgency that should fill us to follow the Lord's commandments. Looking back at the rest of the Exodus story, if the Israelites had delayed their exit from Egypt, the armies of Pharaoh would have caught up to them and slaughtered them.

This seven-day feast was also a time of convocation or gathering and teaching (see Exodus 12:16). In that sense, it was like conference time in our day, when the heavens are open, so to speak, and we feast in the word of God. To the Israelites, this was a time of deep gratitude as they remembered not just their release from over four hundred years of captivity but also how the destroying angel had passed over their forefathers. No doubt this aura of remembrance and gratitude humbled them and prepared them to receive the word of the Lord in a way that we would do well to emulate.

The sacrificial lamb itself was also an important part of the Passover feast. The families were commanded to eat the meat of the sacrificed lamb in a foreshadowing of the sacrament. The circumcised (those who had entered into covenant and were members of the Lamb's Church) were commanded to consume all of the Passover meal (see Exodus 12:10), just as the sacrament is to fill us now (see 3 Nephi 18:9). In fact, the Savior instituted the sacrament at the time of the Passover (see Matthew 26:17–20, 26–28). He and His disciples were actually observing the Passover tradition at the time of the Last Supper. At that moment, the Passover feast that had been symbolically carried out for centuries was fulfilled. The sacrament is nothing less than the fulfillment of the Passover meal.

In all respects, the Passover feast was a striking symbol of the Savior. From the blood of the Lamb to the modern ordinance of the sacrament and the remembrance and gratitude that filled the whole celebration, the symbols of the Savior are unmistakable.

The Feast of Pentecost

Pentecost is best remembered in our day as a New Testament event and not so much as an Old Testament tradition. When we speak of Pentecost, we are more familiar with the outpouring of the Spirit and the mass conversion that occurred in chapter two of Acts. This New Testament occasion has earned its place in history, but it can actually be better understood in light of the Old Testament events of Pentecost.

The Feast of Pentecost was also known as the Feast of the Harvest, the Feast of Weeks, and the Feast of the Firstfruits. The name "Pentecost" is derived from the Greek word for "fifty." The feast earned this name because it was set on the fiftieth day after the beginning of the Feast of the Passover (see Leviticus 23:16). More specifically, this day came seven Sabbaths (49 days) and one day after the beginning of the Passover Feast (see Leviticus 23:15–16).

Pentecost as a Commemoration of Sinai

While Leviticus doesn't mention it, it is generally believed that this is the same fifty-day period that marked Moses receiving the ten commandments on Mount Sinai.[3] At first glance, this feast seems to be purely a celebration of receiving the law, but Moses's experience on Sinai was much more involved. Many Israelites understood that the purpose of that law was to help them, whereas today many people view commandments as a restriction. They also recognized this act of receiving the law as an act of communion with God (see Nehemiah 9:13). For this reason, Sinai was regarded as holy ground (see Psalms 68:8). It was the mountain where God communed with man, where man and God met. For this reason, Donald W. Parry has called Sinai a temple, which would make the Sinai experience a temple experience.[4]

The Sinai experience fits in the Exodus story as one of the essential ordinances in the plan of salvation, taking us out of the world and back toward the presence of God. As we've seen, the Israelites began in Egypt, representing the world. They crossed the Red Sea, representing baptism. In the wilderness by a cloud and pillar of fire, representing the Holy Ghost, as they journeyed through the wilderness back to God. When they received the law and communed with God on Sinai, this represented their temple experience. This experience prepared them to eventually enter the promised land, symbolic of the celestial kingdom.

With this in mind, Moses's receiving the law on Sinai was really just a part of a much greater experience on Sinai: the temple experience of man communing with God. Pentecost may, therefore, be seen as an ancient celebration of the temple.

Pentecost as a Celebration of the Harvest

While the feast was clearly a celebration of the Sinai experience, it was also a day of gratitude, particularly for the blessings of the harvest. The Hebrew texts that describe this feast refer it as the "feast of the harvest" or the "day of the first fruits."

> Six days thou shalt eat unleavened bread; and on the seventh day shall be a solemn assembly to the Lord thy God; thou shalt do no work therein.
>
> Seven weeks shalt thou number unto thee: begin to number the seven weeks from such time as thou beginnest to put the sickle to the corn.
>
> And thou shalt keep the feast of weeks unto the Lord thy God with a tribute of a freewill offering of thine hand, which thou shalt give unto the Lord thy God, according as the Lord thy God hath blessed thee:
>
> And thou shalt rejoice before the Lord thy God, thou, and thy son,

> and thy daughter, and thy manservant, and thy maidservant, and the Levite that is within thy gates, and the stranger, and the fatherless, and the widow, that are among you, in the place which the Lord thy God hath chosen to place his name there.
>
> And thou shalt remember that thou wast a bondman in Egypt: and thou shalt observe and do these statutes (Deuteronomy 16:8–12).

Once again, we see that the theme of this feast was gratitude and remembrance. This particular feast was based on the gratitude the Israelites felt for the harvest that sustained them, just as the manna from heaven and water from the rock had done when they were traveling in the wilderness.

The Link among the Commemorations of Pentecost

Pentecost is now remembered as a commemoration of three separate great events. The first is the New Testament day when the Spirit of the Lord was poured out overwhelmingly, following His forty-day ministry after the Resurrection. The second commemoration is of the Lord's appearance to Moses on Mount Sinai for the benefit of the Israelites. The third commemoration is of the Old Testament celebration of the completed harvest. Each of these three commemorations points to the Savior.

The outpouring of the Spirit in chapter two of Acts was a celebration of the Savior. This was the fulfillment of the Savior's promise to pour out the Holy Ghost on His followers (see John 14:26; 15:26; Moroni 4:3; 5:2; D&C 20:77, 79). The Sinai experience was the premortal Savior appearing to His prophet Moses and was symbolic of the temple experience that is available to all worthy adult members of the Lord's restored Church. The harvest was a celebration of the physical sustenance received by the Israelites and the spiritual sustenance it was meant to symbolize. That sustenance comes from the Savior, who makes eternal life possible. Through all of these facets and types of Christ, the theme of gratitude and remembrance predominates.

The Feast of Tabernacles

The third mandatory feast was the Feast of Tabernacles or the Feast of Booths. It gains its name from the "booths" or temporary housing in which the Israelites lived while in the wilderness for forty years. While the Passover was a commemoration of the Lord's mercy in liberating Israel from Egypt, the Feast of Tabernacles was a commemoration of the Lord's mercy to the Israelites after their escape from Egypt. After all, their liberation would not have been a complete blessing without the Lord's sustaining power in the wilderness where they journeyed for forty years before they could enter the promised land. And they readily recognized this.

This feast came five days after the Day of Atonement. This places it in a time of particular "cleanliness" for the Israelites "when the sins of the chosen people had been removed and when their special covenant relation to Jehovah had been renewed and restored."[5]

Of all the feasts, this one was most purely based on rejoicing and praising the Lord. This feast was entirely focused on gratitude and remembering the how the Lord sustained the Israelites for their forty years in the wilderness and blessed them upon their eventual entry into the promised land of Canaan. "The fact that it celebrated the completion of the full harvest symbolizes the gospel reality that it is the mission of the house of Israel to gather all nations to Jehovah, a process that is now going forward, but will not be completed until that millennial day when 'the Lord shall be king over all the earth,' and shall reign personally thereon."[6]

This feast was also marked with sacrifices. In fact, on the day of this feast more sacrifices of bullocks, rams, lambs, and goats were offered by the priests than during all the other Israelite feasts combined.[7]

Interestingly, this feast is also the origin of the "hosanna shout" that is practiced with the dedication of temples in the latter days.[8] Anciently, palm branches were waved, and even though these have now been replaced with white handkerchiefs, the purpose of greeting the Lord remains the same. This practice was fulfilled when the Savior entered Jerusalem in the last few days of His mortal ministry. "On the next day much people that were come to the feast, when they heard that Jesus was coming to Jerusalem, took branches of palm trees, and went forth to meet him, and cried, Hosanna: Blessed is the King of Israel that cometh in the name of the Lord" (John 12:12–13; see also Matthew 21:8–9). Some of those who had been celebrating this feast realized its purpose and fulfillment when they recognized their Messiah entering Jerusalem, the very place they had been commanded to assemble for the Feast of Tabernacles.

Unfortunately far too few people recognized the true purpose and focal point of their feast when He appeared before their own eyes. Again, gratitude and remembrance are the themes of this great feast. When the very subject of that gratitude and remembrance appeared before the eyes of some understanding Israelites, they recognized their Messiah.

The Timing of Sacred Days Pointing to Christ

The most sacred times of the year for Israelites have always been Passover and Yom Kippur, the Day of Atonement. The meaning and practices of these days unquestionably point to Christ, but the lessons do not end with the outward ordinances. The days themselves point to Christ.

Nisan and Tishri

The lunar Jewish calendar is remarkable in that it has two separate beginnings and reckoning points: an ecclesiastical one and a civil one. The ecclesiastical calendar begins with the month known as Nisan, while the civil calendar begins with the month Tishri. Nisan is believed by some to be the month or the time at which the universe was created, while Tishri is held in tradition to be the time Adam and Eve were created. While Nisan is the first month on the ecclesiastical calendar, it is the seventh month on the civil calendar. Likewise, Tishri is the first month on the civil calendar and the seventh month on the ecclesiastical calendar. The seventh month was usually the middle point of the year, except that the Jewish calendar sometimes had a thirteenth month for the same reason that we have leap years under our Gregorian calendar—a full year is not perfectly divisible in whole numbers of days.

With regard to the three feasts that the Israelites were commanded to travel to Jerusalem to observe, Passover falls in Nisan, Pentecost falls fifty days after Passover and thus is reckoned from Nisan, and the Feast of Tabernacles falls in Tishri.

If we were to graph and superimpose these ecclesiastical and civil calendars in chiastic form as we did with the earth's history, it would look like this:

Ecclesiastical Calendar	**Civil Calendar**
NISAN	TISHRI
TISHRI	NISAN
ADAR[9]	ELUL[10]

The ecclesiastical and civil calendars, when overlapped, form a chiasmus with each significant month being the beginning of one calendar and the middle point of the other calendar.

How Does This Point to Christ?

Christ is both a priest and a king. That means He is both an ecclesiastical and civil ruler. The two reckonings are dependent on each other. He stands at the both the head and the middle of each reckoning of time. Under both methods of measuring temporal existence, the Lord is both the beginning and the focal point.

Passover

The Passover celebration covered separate and distinct days that, as we just discussed, commemorated separate and distinct events that were essential to the liberation of Israel (representing the Lord's covenant people) from Egypt (representing the captivity of the world).

Before the Passover began, the Passover lamb was chosen on 10 Nisan. That lamb was sacrificed on 14 Nisan, the day marking when the firstborns throughout Egypt died while the Israelites who had applied the blood of the lamb to their doorposts were all spared. On 15 Nisan, Pharaoh allowed the Israelites to leave Egypt. This was the day of feasting in commemoration of the end of slavery under the Egyptians. The next day, 16 Nisan, was a day of celebration when the first fruits of the harvest were brought forth and presented to the Lord.

LDS historian John L. Pratt has researched and pinpointed these specific dates at the time of the Savior's crucifixion.[11] His conclusion includes not only an exact date on our Gregorian calendar when these events took place, but a remarkable set of parallels between the Hebrew festival days and the events of the Savior's last week in mortality. According to Pratt, the Passover activities perfectly prefigured the events that took place during the Savior's last week, a week that is central to the salvation of mankind.

The day on which the Passover lamb was chosen was the same day that the Lamb of God was "chosen" with His triumphal entry into Jerusalem and hailed as the Messiah (see Matthew 21:1–9; Mark 11:1–11; Luke 19:37–40; John 12:12–13). The day when the Passover lamb was sacrificed was the same day that the Lamb of God, the Savior of mankind, was sacrificed on the cross (see John 19:31).

The day on which Israel celebrated liberation from Egypt was the day when the Lamb of God "liberated" the spirits in spirit prison. "For Christ also hath once suffered for sins, the just for the unjust, that he might bring us to God, being put to death in the flesh, but quickened by the Spirit: By which also he went and preached unto the spirits in prison" (1 Peter 3:18–19). This liberation was the part of the Savior's mission as prophesied by Isaiah to "proclaim liberty to the captives, and the opening of the prison doors to them that are bound" (Isaiah 61:1). It was also part of the ministry that He Himself proclaimed (see Luke 4:18–21).

The day on which the first fruits of the Hebrews' harvest were brought forth was the same day on which the first fruits of the resurrection came forth (see Jacob 4:11).

In chart form, these events are as follows:

Date (AD 33)	**Judean Day**	**Passover Event**	**Event in the Savior's Life**
Monday, March 28	10 Nisan	Passover lamb chosen	Messiah chosen during triumphal entry
Friday, April 1	14 Nisan	Passover lamb sacrificed	Lamb of God Sacrificed
Saturday, April 2	15 Nisan	Israel freed from Egypt	Liberation preached to captives in spirit prison
Sunday, April 3	16 Nisan	first fruits of harvest	first fruits of resurrection come forth

There is no coincidence to be found here. The Old Testament practices perfectly prefigured the Savior's victory over sin and death, right down to the date.

Passover and the Return of Elijah

John Pratt's study also points out that in the year of the Savior's crucifixion, 16 Nisan fell on Sunday, April 3. This first Easter was the same date on which Elijah returned in the Kirtland temple in 1836 (see D&C 110).

Even today, it is customary among the Jews to set an extra space at the table for Elijah when they sit down for the Passover meal. Elijah's return, foretold in the Old Testament (see Malachi 4:5–6), is anxiously anticipated, but it has in fact already happened. The longstanding belief was that Elijah would return on Passover, and, in fact, he did exactly that.[12]

You may be wondering, of all days, why April 3 (16 Nisan)? According to Pratt:

> The Prophet Joseph Smith explained that 'the spirit of Elias is first, Elijah second, and Messiah last. Elias [who also came to the Kirtland temple to restore priesthood keys] is a forerunner to prepare the way, and the spirit and power of Elijah is to come after, holding the keys of power, building the Temple to the capstone, placing the seals of the Melchizedek Priesthood upon the house of Israel, and making all things ready; then Messiah comes to His Temple, which is last of all.
>
> Thus, the coming of Elijah on 3 April 1836 was to occur after the forerunners had returned in the spirit of Elias to prepare the way. [see D&C 27:6–7; D&C 128:20–21]. At his return, Elijah declared: "Therefore, the keys of this dispensation are committed into your hands; and by this ye may know that the great and dreadful day of the Lord is near, even at the doors" [D&C 110:16]. With the keys of the dispensation of the fulness of times restored [see D&C 112:30], the Church would then "build up the kingdom before the coming of the great day of the Lord."[13]

The timing of Elijah's return on the day of the Lord's Resurrection is also a reminder of the pathway to eternal life that is provided in the temple, where the sealing keys restored by Elijah are administered. As the Savior's Resurrection broke the bands of death and paved the way for all mankind to conquer the grave, the ordinances of the temple allow us full access to the Atonement so that we may gain eternal life.

Yom Kippur

Notwithstanding the marvelous celebration of the Passover, Yom Kippur—the Day of Atonement—has always been regarded as the most sacred day of the Hebrew calendar. Both days prefigure the events of the Atonement. While Passover prefigures the very date of the atoning events, Yom Kippur, as the Day of Atonement, prefigures the *title* and *substance* of those events.

On Yom Kippur the high priest entered the Holy of Holies and applied the blood of the lamb to the mercy seat (or atonement cover, according to the footnote on Exodus 25:17) for the redemption of Israel. The Holy of Holies and the mercy seat on the ark of the covenant represented the presence of God Himself, and the blood of the lamb obviously represented the blood of the Lamb of God. This was a day of cleansing and purification for all of Israel. This is an unmistakable type of the Savior's Atonement, as it cleanses and purifies those who repent and are baptized and adopted into the House of Israel.

The Day of Atonement comes on 10 Tishri—exactly half a year after the Passover week. Tishri, the month of Yom Kippur, is the first month of the civil year and the seventh month of the ecclesiastical year. Nisan, the month of the Passover festivities, is the first month of the ecclesiastical year and the seventh month of the civil year. The key days within each month correspond to each other as a mirror image. They are each other's "general conference," with Passover roughly corresponding to April conference, and the Day of Atonement roughly corresponding to October conference. They are each other's solstices and equinoxes. They each represent the meridian of time for that year, in both ecclesiastical and civil terms. This means they are each not just the center point but also the "high noon," so to speak, of the year.

Why would the Lord set two separate times diametrically opposed to each other to prefigure the Atonement? The answers may be countless. The timing of the two dates may be a lesson on building our lives around the Atonement and letting the Atonement surround and envelop our lives, just as the two symbolic days surround the rest of the year, and the rest of the year perfectly surrounds the two holy days.

It may also be a lesson on reconciling the temporal (as illustrated by the civil calendar) with the spiritual (as illustrated by the ecclesiastical calendar). This may be a reminder of the blessings of being both a king (a civil leader) and a priest (an ecclesiastical leader). The blessings of exaltation that come through the Atonement are described as a bestowal of both these titles that are borne by the Savior (see D&C 76:56).

The timing may also be symbolic of the Savior's coming in the meridian of time (see Moses 5:57; 6:57, 62; 7:46; D&C 20:26; 39:3), as each day is the "meridian" of the year, by either the civil or ecclesiastical reckoning. It may also be that the events of the two days emphasize different lessons about the Atonement. The Passover may be seen as emphasizing the role of the priest in the tabernacle, who offered the sacrifice. At the same time, Yom Kippur may be seen as emphasizing the priests' application of the blood in the presence of God on behalf of the people to make them worthy of His presence.

Passover may likewise be seen as emphasizing the blessings of salvation and redemption from death, while Yom Kippur may be seen as emphasizing the blessings of exaltation and entering the presence of God. It may also be showing that the Savior's Atonement is so vast and far-reaching that it really cannot be explained in only one lesson or fit into only one day. It could even be fairly stated that the Atonement is captured in all of the Savior's life, not just Gethsemane or Golgotha. After all, it was His entire life that qualified Him as the sacrificial lamb and enabled Him to atone for our sins. And it was His entire life that provided a perfect example for mankind. Without that example to follow, forgiveness would be of little use, since we could never grow by following in the footsteps that lead to eternal life.

The list of lessons from these sacred days may go on and on. This is the marvel of symbolism and the marvel of the Atonement. Our mortal minds can only begin to understand the Savior's Atonement, as depicted and prefigured by the feasts of the Mosaic law.

Notes

1. LDS Bible Dictionary, 708.
2. McConkie, *The Promised Messiah*, 429.
3. S. Kent Brown & Richard Neitzel Holzapfel, *Between the Testaments* (Salt Lake City: Deseret Book, 2002), 226.
   See also Genesis 19:1.
4. Donald W. Parry, "Sinai as Sanctuary and Mountain of God" accessed via GospeLink.com, also published in *By Study and Also by Faith*, vol. 1, ed. John M. Lundquist & Stephen D. Ricks (Salt

Lake City: Shadow Mountain, 1990), 482–500.

Jacob Milgrom has also compared the Sinai experience to the ancient tabernacle, the forerunner of the modern restored temple. He said,

> Mount Sinai is the archetype of the Tabernacle, and is similarly divided into three gradations of holiness. Its summit is the Holy of Holies; God's voice issues forth from there (Exodus 19:20) as from the inner shrine (Exodus 25:22; Numbers 7:89); the mountaintop is off limits to priest and layman alike (Exodus 19:24) and its very sight is punishable by death (Exodus 19:21), and so with its Tabernacle counterpart (cf. Leviticus 16:2 and Numbers 4:20); finally, Moses alone is privileged to ascend to the top (Exodus 19:20; see 34:2) just as later, the high priest is permitted to enter the inner shrine under special safeguards (Leviticus 16:2–4). The second division of Sinai is the equivalent of the outer shrine, marked off from the rest of the mountain by being enveloped in a cloud (Exodus 20:21; 24:15–18) just as the cloud overspreads the entirety of the Tabernacle (Numbers 9:1522). . . . Below the cloud is the third division. . . . Here is where the altar and stelae are erected (Exodus 24:4). It is equivalent to the courtyard, the sacred enclosure of the Tabernacle.

From Jacob Milgrom *Studies in Levitical Terminology*, (Berkeley, CA: University of California Press, 1970), 44–45; as quoted by Parry, "Sinai as Sanctuary," accessed via GospeLink.com.

5. McConkie, *The Promised Messiah*, 432.
6. Ibid., 433.
7. Ibid.
8. Ibid., 433–34.
9. This was the twelfth month of the ecclesiastical year and sixth month of the civil year. To account for a full year, a thirteenth month, Adar II or Veadar was periodically added.
10. This was the sixth month of the year on the ecclesiastical calendar and the twelfth month of the year on the civil calendar.
11. John L. Pratt, "The Restoration of Priesthood Keys on Easter 1836, Part 1: Dating the First Easter," *Ensign*, June 1985, 59; "The Restoration of Priesthood Keys on Easter 1836, Part 2: Symbolism of Passover and of Elijah's Return," *Ensign*, July 1985, 55.

Part One of this series also dates the Savior's birth at April 6, as proposed in the "Earth" chapter. Significantly, Pratt's study also places the Savior's birth in the year 1 BC, a date that he convincingly substantiates through biblical and Book of Mormon records. Elder James E. Talmage concurs with this date, as also noted in the "Earth" chapter. In fact, it appears that these conclusions could be little more than a hypothesis without the records kept by Book of Mormon prophets. This may be yet another reason to treasure the Book of Mormon.

12. Pratt, "The Restoration of Priesthood Keys, Part 2," *Ensign*, July, 1985.
13. Ibid.

The Prophets

Through prophets, we receive the word of God. All prophets since the beginning of time have shared the common purpose of bearing witness of Jesus (see Luke 1:70; Acts 10:43). "And I said unto him: Believest thou the scriptures? And he said, Yea. And I said unto him: Then ye do not understand them; for they truly testify of Christ. Behold I say unto you that none of the prophets have written, nor prophesied, save they have spoken concerning this Christ" (Jacob 7:10–11). Besides teaching and testifying of Christ, the prophets and the scriptures that come through them also typify and symbolize Him.

The Book of Mormon and Jesus Christ

As a starting point, consider the Book of Mormon. There is no question that this book teaches and testifies of Christ throughout its pages. However, consider also the parallels between the book itself and the Savior of whom it testifies:[1]

- Both were declared by an angel as they came forth.
- Both came to restore the gospel in the time of apostasy.
- Both ushered in a new dispensation.
- Both were laid away in a stone receptacle, waiting to come forth again by the power of God.
- The Book of Mormon was taken from the stone receptacle by Joseph Smith. The Savior was put into a stone tomb by Joseph of Arimathaea.

- Both came forth from their stone receptacle after a stone was rolled away.
- An angel oversaw both coming forth from the stone receptacle.
- Joseph Smith, the first one to see the Book of Mormon after it came forth, was forbidden to touch it. Mary, the first one to see the Savior after He came forth, was forbidden to touch Him.
- The Book of Mormon was engraved in gold, a most precious metal that never loses its brightness. Christ is the most precious being, and He never loses His brightness.
- Both the Book of Mormon and the Savior were attested to by twelve witnesses.
- Both are the word (or Word) of God.
- Both teach the fulness of the gospel.
- The Book of Mormon is the keystone of our religion. Christ is the cornerstone of the Church.
- Both speak again after coming forth from the ground or grave.
- Both were received by the poor and the meek (see Isaiah 29:19).
- Both open spiritual eyes and ears (see Isaiah 29:18; Matthew 13:16–17).
- Both bring understanding and doctrine (see Isaiah 29:24).
- Both were taken away to be revealed again.
- Both were to return to reveal all things (see 2 Nephi 27:11; D&C 101:32).
- The Book of Mormon causes the children of Jacob to sanctify the Holy One of Jacob (see Isaiah 29:23). Christ is the Holy one of Jacob (see 2 Nephi 25:29).

Notice the prevalence of stone or rocks in these parallels. We would not normally think of stone as a source of life, but both the Book of Mormon and the resurrected Savior came forth from stone into new life. In all these respects, the Book of Mormon not only bears witness of Christ, but it quite literally typifies Him.

Prophets as Direct Types of Christ

To some extent, all prophets called since the beginning of time have been types of the Savior. Some of these prophets and great people in the scriptures mirror the Savior in so many ways that their lives and missions embody specific missions of the Savior. For example, Jonah is an obvious representation of the Savior's Resurrection. He spent three days in the belly of the great fish to emerge rededicated to serving the Lord on a mission to Nineveh (see Jonah 1–3; Matthew 12:38–41). Likewise, the Apostle Peter's own name, as dubbed by the Savior Himself, is a reference to the Savior, as it means "rock" and "foundation" in Greek (see Matthew 16:18; John 1:42). The Savior is the Rock, the Stone of Israel, the only sure foundation on which men may build. (see Helaman 5:12; 2 Nephi 4:30; 1 Corinthians 3:11; 10:4; D&C 50:44; D&C 128:10).

Many prophets have been called on to follow the example of the Lord by sealing their testimony of the Savior with their own blood. Ten of the original twelve disciples were martyred.[2] Stephen (see Acts 7:59–60), Abinadi (see Mosiah 17:7–15), Gideon (see Alma 1:8–9), and Joseph and Hyrum Smith (see D&C 135) all likewise sealed their testimonies with their own blood. Even the Savior's mother, Mary, was a typification of Christ. Her name in Hebrew, *Marah*, means "bitter," a prophecy and description of the sufferings of her Son (3 Nephi 11:11).[3]

Many other prophets served as types and shadows of Christ not by the manner of their death but by the manner of their lives. They served as living prophecies of the Savior.

Adam

The entire theme of gospel symbolism is using the physical to teach of the spiritual. Perhaps no prophet exemplifies this principle more thoroughly than Adam. Adam prefigured Christ by being the earthly father of mankind. In fact, the name or word "Adam" means "mankind."[4] In this sense, "Adam" is a generic term used for all of humanity, including both men and women. Christ is the spiritual father of mankind through covenants made in His name (see Mosiah 5:7–8). This is at least part of the reason why Paul referred to Christ as the second or last Adam.

> And so it is written, The first man Adam was made a living soul; *the last Adam was made a quickening spirit.*
>
> Howbeit that was not first which is spiritual, but that which is natural; and afterward that which is spiritual.
>
> The first man is of the earth, earthy: *the second man is the Lord from heaven.*

> As is the earthy, such are they also that are earthy: and as is the heavenly, such are they also that are heavenly.
>
> And as we have borne the image of the earthy, we shall also bear the image of the heavenly. (1 Corinthians 15:45–49, emphasis added)

Within Adam and Christ, the physical is used to teach of the eternal. As we learned earlier, the mortality that came through Father Adam is the bridge that leads to our Heavenly Father.

Adam is also known as Michael. It was his premortal name.[5] We learn from the Doctrine and Covenants that it is also his postmortal name (see D&C 27:11; 78:16). This is significant because the name "Michael" literally means "who is like God" in Hebrew.[6] If we map this progression as we have in other chapters, it looks like this:

MICHAEL—Who is like God
    ADAM—Mankind on Earth
MICHAEL—Who is like God

How does this point to Christ? It illustrates man's divine origin and man's potential through the Atonement of Jesus Christ. Mapping this progression further looks like this:

MICHAEL—Who is like God
    ADAM—Mankind after the Fall—CHRIST—The Atonement reverses the Fall
MICHAEL—Mankind having applied the Atonement to become again like God

By typifying mankind's origin and potential, Adam actually represents the most prolific symbol of Christ of all; he represents us. In being reborn through the waters of baptism, we begin the journey to becoming again like Christ. As part of that same journey, we take upon ourselves His name (see D&C 20:37). This is not a name to be taken lightly. As our children take our earthly names, this is a heavenly name that makes us His if we honor it. By following in the footsteps of Adam through the waters of baptism and back to the tree of life, we too can become like God, whose name we bear.

Abraham

Like Christ, Abraham went to and was later delivered from Egypt (see Abraham 2). As we are to do, Abraham made the most of his time in Egypt (representing the world) by learning, teaching and earning the respect of others (see Abraham 3; Facsimile 3).

However, the most symbolic experience in Abraham's life—and perhaps even in all of scripture—was the sacrifice of his son Isaac. In this symbolic representation of the Atonement, we may think that Abraham was acting strictly as a type for Heavenly Father, while Isaac was the type for Christ. However, the symbolism doesn't end there. Abraham's participation also parallels Christ's role in that Abraham was the offerer (as the father of Isaac) and the priest (who was to slay the sacrificial animal). As we discussed before, these are both roles of the Savior. Therefore, Abraham's test on Mount Moriah is a type of both the Father and the Son.

In the scriptures the term "only begotten son" is used to describe only two people: The Savior Himself and Isaac (see John 1:14, 18; 3:16; Hebrews 11:17). As the Father offered His Only Begotten for the salvation of all His children who would repent and obey, Abraham was commanded to offer his only begotten as perhaps the most poignant lesson on the Atonement imaginable.

Much like Adam before him, Abraham did not know why he was commanded to offer this sacrifice, but he knew that the Lord had commanded it (see Moses 5:6). Abraham and his son marched up to Mount Moriah (see Genesis 22:2). This same place was later the site of Solomon's temple (see 2 Chonicles 3:1). In turn, Solomon's temple was the forerunner of the modern temple that makes all the blessings of the Atonement available to mankind. Abraham and Isaac carried with them the wood to burn the sacrifice, but only Abraham knew at the time that Isaac was the sacrifice to be offered (see Genesis 22:7–8).

When Isaac learned that he would be the sacrifice, there is no indication in Genesis that he protested. We can only tell that he accepted this divine appointment to die with willingness to fulfill a will greater than his own. Without question, the great patriarch Isaac was a model of obedience and eternal perspective, just like the Savior Himself. Perhaps Isaac even understood that he was to be sacrificed not in spite of his status as the only begotten but *because* of that status.

When Abraham "stretched forth his hand, and took the knife to slay his son" (Genesis 22:10), an angel intervened, calling Abraham by name (see Genesis 22:11). Abraham responded by echoing the words of the premortal Savior, "Here am I" (Genesis 22:11; Abraham 3:27). In response to this unfailing obedience, the divine reprieve was given. "Lay not thine hand upon the lad, neither do thou any thing unto him: for now I know that thou hast feared God, seeing thou hast not withheld thy son, thine only son from me" (Genesis 22:12). At this point, the sacrifice of a broken or completely willing heart and a contrite spirit was enough, and Abraham was not ultimately required to sacrifice Isaac.

This sacrifice of a broken heart and a contrite spirit is the same sacrifice required of us (see 3 Nephi 9:19–20). Perhaps we can judge whether we are truly offering this sacrifice by comparing ourselves to Abraham on Mount Moriah and asking if we are also willing to give the Lord anything He requires.

In contrast to this similitude, the Only Begotten of the Father was not spared on Golgotha. There was no ram in the thicket when it was the Savior's turn on the cross. The Messiah alone could atone for the sins of mankind. While Abraham and Isaac's faith and obedience were enough on Mount Moriah, faith and obedience were not enough on Golgotha. Our own guilt required the sacrifice of the Lamb of God.

However, like Abraham and Isaac, faith and obedience, exemplified by a broken heart and contrite spirit, are enough for you and me to gain the reward of what happened on Golgotha. That faith and obedience will lead us to our own Mount Moriah, the mountain of the Lord's house, where we offer our hearts as a sacrifice through covenant, and where the Atonement is fully accessed.

Joseph

Of all Old Testament prophets who foreshadowed the Savior, Joseph is perhaps the most specific type and shadow of Christ.

- Joseph was a firstborn entitled to the birthright blessings in a family line of great patriarchs (see Genesis 30:22–24; 43:33); Jesus was the Firstborn of the Father (see D&C 93:21).
- Both Joseph and Jesus were shepherds (see Genesis 37:2; John 10:11).

- Both were especially and uniquely loved by their fathers (see Genesis 37:3; Matthew 3:17).
- Both were unjustly hated by their brothers and peers (see Genesis 37:4; John 15:25).
- Both were sent to reign but were rejected (see Genesis 37:8; Luke 19:14).
- Both were stripped of their robes by their brethren as part of their betrayal (see Genesis 37:23; Matthew 27:28).
- Both were sold for the price of a slave. In Joseph's day, that was twenty pieces of silver (see Genesis 37:28). In Christ's day, that was thirty pieces of silver (see Matthew 26:15).
- Judah wanted to sell Joseph for profit (see Genesis 37:26–27). Christ was betrayed and sold by Judas, which is simply the Greek form of the same name (see Matthew 27:3).
- Both were sent to Egypt to live because they were seen as a threat (see Genesis 37:28; Matthew 2:13).
- Both managed to find favor despite their lowly beginnings; Joseph began as a servant in Potiphar's house (see Genesis 39:1–6), and Christ began His life in a manger (see Luke 2:7, 12).
- Both were unjustly accused and punished (see Genesis 39:12–20; Matthew 26:59–67; 27:1–50).
- Both were wrongfully imprisoned or punished with two others (see Genesis 40:2–3; Luke 23:32–33).
- Somehow, even in the darkest times of their wrongful punishments, both offered encouragement and love to those who were accused with them (see Genesis 40:13; Luke 23:43).
- Both began their formal ministries at the age of thirty (see Genesis 41:46; Luke 3:23).
- Both were so trusted in their positions that their subjects were instructed to do whatever they said (see Genesis 41:55; John 2:5).
- Both were unrecognized even by their own brethren (see Genesis 42–43; Isaiah 53:2; 3 Nephi 9:16).
- Eventually, both were recognized or yet will be recognized by their brethren (see Genesis 45:1, 12; Luke 24:31, 39; Isaiah 45:23; Romans 14:11; Mosiah 27:31; D&C 88:104).
- In some of the most ironic twists in history, both became the means of salvation, even to those who had betrayed them (see

Genesis 45:7; Hebrews 5:9). In the case of the Savior, I would dare call it *the* most ironic twist in history.
- Both performed their works of salvation by symbolically or literally purchasing their brethren from the throes of death (see Genesis 47:23; 1 Corinthians 6:19–20).

The theme of Egypt is prominent in other prophetic types of Christ. Again, Egypt represents the world and its powers of captivity. Overcoming Egypt is a central theme of many prophets' lives and fits well within the central theme of gospel symbolism, which is to learn the spiritual or eternal from the physical or worldly.

The Savior told us, "These things I have spoken unto you, that in me ye might have peace. In the world ye shall have tribulation: but be of good cheer; I have overcome the world" (John 16:33; see also D&C 50:41). Joseph symbolically overcame Egypt and the world by prospering in it through his faithfulness, diligence, loyalty, and obedience, even after he had been wrongfully accused. This gave him honor in the eyes of those who would otherwise have been his enemies.

This summarizes our goal in mortality: To overcome the world. "For verily I say unto you, I will [meaning want] that ye should overcome the world; wherefore I will have compassion upon you" (D&C 64:2). As with Joseph, our key to overcoming the world is faithfulness, for "he that is faithful and endureth shall overcome the world" (D&C 63:47).

Moses

Joseph directly links to Moses, as Joseph specifically prophesied of Moses. Joseph foretold, "For a seer I will raise up to deliver my people out of the land of Egypt; and he shall be called Moses" (JST—Genesis 50:29). As if that prophecy were not clear enough, the Lord continued through Joseph, "And by this name he shall know that he is of thy house; for he shall be nursed by the king's daughter, and shall be called her son" (JST—Genesis 50:29).

Like Joseph, Moses would be a living type of Christ in many ways.

- Both Moses and Christ were raised by a sort of adoptive earthly parent (see Exodus 2:10; Luke 3:23).
- Both Moses and Christ were spared from the orders of wicked kings

to kill male children because the kings viewed them as a threat to their tyrannical powers (see Exodus 1:22; Matthew 2:16).

- Both were lawgivers (see Exodus 20; Matthew 5:17; 3 Nephi 15:1–10).
- Moses overcame Egypt (see Exodus 14), which is a scriptural symbol of the world, and Christ overcame the world (see D&C 50:41).
- In overcoming the world, both led their people out of bondage. Moses's people escaped physical bondage, while the children of Christ are led from the bondage of sin and death (see Alma 22:14).

Without taking anything away from these parallels, the greatest symbolic lesson about the Savior that came from Moses was the Mosaic law. The law of Moses was given as a schoolmaster to bring the people to Christ (see Galatians 3:24). As we have already seen, the law, and particularly the sacrifices and feasts it required, prepared people for Christ's coming by foreshadowing the Atonement and His mission. The law was specifically designed to typify Christ and point the people to His coming. Christ's coming marked the fulfillment of the Mosaic law (see Matthew 5:17). He added to the law with teachings that took the people closer to heaven. Simply put, the law of Moses pointed or brought the people to Christ. Christ's role is to then deliver His people to the Father (see John 17:3).

Moses is frequently mentioned together with his companion, Aaron. In Aaron, and in those holders of the priesthood named for him, we see the same kind of preparation or deliverance that we see in Moses and the law named for him. The Aaronic Priesthood is sometimes called the preparatory priesthood. Just as the Mosaic law led to Christ, the Aaronic Priesthood leads to the Melchizedek Priesthood. The Melchizedek Priesthood represents Christ, which we know because it was originally called the Holy Priesthood, after the Order of the Son of God (see D&C 107:3).

This same theme of deliverance and preparation is evident in some instructions that were given to Levi, whose descendants were administrators of the Aaronic Priesthood. The apocryphal Testament of Levi records a visit between the Lord and Levi in which the Lord instructs, "Levi, I have given thee the blessings of the priesthood until I come and sojourn in the midst of Israel." In this respect, the lesser priesthood was given specifically "until [the Lord] come[s] and sojourn[s] in the midst of Israel."

This explanation of Levi's priesthood follows the same pattern: The Aaronic or Levitical Priesthood (see D&C 107:6) was given in order to carry Israel through until the Lord's coming in the flesh. With the Restoration, the Aaronic Priesthood was given at least in part to carry modern-day Israel through until the Lord's second coming (see D&C 13).

In all these instances, the Aaronic Priesthood leads directly to Jesus Christ, His Priesthood, and His reign on earth. This is a perfect parallel with the Mosaic law, which was specifically intended to bring the people to Christ and prepared them for His coming.

Joshua

The Mosaic law did not have the power to bring people back to the presence of God. That simply was not its purpose. The purpose of the Mosaic law was to bring people to Christ. It is Christ who has the power to save and to bring His people back to the presence of God. This purpose was illustrated in the Exodus story. Moses led the Israelites out of bondage through the waters of the Red Sea (symbolic of the ordinance of baptism, which is administered by the Aaronic Priesthood) and through the wilderness.

However, Moses never got to lead the Israelites into the promised land. It was not his role, just as it was not the role of the law named after him or the priesthood named after his brother, Aaron.

The role and honor of delivering the Israelites into the promised land belonged to Joshua, who again is a direct type and shadow of Christ. Joshua's name, before being anglicized into our King James Bible, was Yehoushua.[7] This is the same name as Jesus, which likewise has been anglicized in our King James Bible. Coming from the Hebrew Old Testament, the name Yehoushua became "Joshua," while the Greek New Testament caused the name to be translated as "Jesus."[8]

In Joshua we see the same role as that played by the Savior: to bring people into the promised land, which represents the celestial kingdom. Again, Moses and his law and corresponding priesthood bring the people to Jesus Christ, and He and His corresponding law and priesthood deliver them to the Father.

Moses and Joshua both had similar experiences as they led the Israelites. They both spoke with God, who told them to take off their shoes because they were on sacred ground (see Exodus 3:5; Joshua 5:15). They both led the Israelites through water that greeted them as dry ground. Moses led the Israelites through the Red Sea and away from Egypt, as a symbolic representation of baptism (see Exodus 14:21–31). Joshua led the Israelites through the Jordan River and into the promised land (see Joshua 3:13–17), as a symbol of the higher ordinances of the gospel. This is yet another lesson on the Savior. The ordinances of the Aaronic Priesthood, such as baptism, have the power to bring people to Christ and membership in His Church. And the power of exaltation lies in the ordinances of the Melchizedek Priesthood, or the Holy Priesthood, after the Order of the Son of God (see D&C 107:3; 84:19–22). This priesthood is required to carry out the higher ordinances of the temple.

Summary

The entire purpose of laws and prophets is to bring us to Christ. In many instances, the law and the prophets personify and embody Christ in addition to testifying of Him. By obeying the laws of Christ, we come unto the Giver of those laws. By receiving prophets, we receive the One who sent them, and by receiving Him, we receive the Father (see Matthew 10:40).

NOTES

1. These observations are from the lessons and lectures of Robert J. Norman, used by permission.
2. John would have suffered the same fate of martyrdom if not for his translated state (D&C 7). Judas also died an untimely death, but he definitely does not qualify as a martyr.
3. Strong, *Strong's Exhaustive Concordance of the Bible,* Hebrew word 4751.
4. Ibid., Hebrew word 120.
   Interestingly, adding the Hebrew suffix "ah" to the root word *adam* makes the word for "earth." (See Strong, *Strong's Exhaustive Concordance of the Bible,* Hebrew word 127.)
5. Bruce R. McConkie, *Doctrines of the Restoration*, (Salt Lake City: Bookcraft, 1989), 84.
6. Strong, *Strong's Exhaustive Concordance of the Bible,* Hebrew word 4317.
7. Ibid., Hebrew word 3091.
8. Ibid., Greek word 2424.

SECTION THREE

Other Prominent Scriptural Symbols

Salt

Salt is a prominent scriptural symbol. "It is essential to health; body cells must have salt in order to live and work. It has antiseptic, or germ-killing, properties. It is a preservative. It is an ingredient in many foods and products. And it is estimated that there are more than fourteen thousand uses for salt."[1]

Salt of the Earth

While salt is prominent in the Creation as part of the oceans, it also holds a separate place as part of the Savior's teachings about righteous people. In the Doctrine and Covenants, the Lord refers to His saints as "the salt of the earth." He says, "When men are called unto mine everlasting gospel, and covenant with an everlasting covenant, they are accounted as the salt of the earth and the savor of men. They are called to be the savor of men; therefore, if that salt of the earth lose its savor, behold, it is thenceforth good for nothing only to be cast out and trodden under the feet of men" (D&C 101:39–40).

In the Sermon on the Mount, as it is clarified in the Joseph Smith Translation and as it was given in the Americas, the Lord also likened His followers to salt, giving them the ability to "become the salt of the earth" (JST—Matthew 5:15; 3 Nephi 12:13).

In this symbolic representation, the message is not conveyed as a creation of Deity such as the earth, trees, or rock; rather, in this instance, the symbolism is conveyed by God's most precious creation: Man. The symbolic lessons conveyed by salt are aimed directly at us. Salt teaches us what roles we should be performing and how we should perform them.

Salt "retards the process of deterioration" and is therefore a symbol of "incorruption and preservation."[2] As a preservative and a seasoning, salt was indispensable to the Hebrews. With that in mind, becoming the "salt of the earth" symbolizes a great responsibility to the Lord's followers. The Savior gave these followers the power to become the preserving and seasoning agents to the rest of the world. They would keep the world from being bland and from spoiling. They would be the source of great blessings unto the rest of the world.

Since the Savior gave unto His followers to "become" rather than to be "the salt of the earth," we can be sure that there is a condition to this blessing. If we look back to the Doctrine and Covenants, we see that the Lord was referring to those who would "suffer persecution" in the Lord's name and "endure in faith, though they are called to lay down their lives for . . . [the Lord's] sake." And yet, these same people will in time "partake of all this glory" (D&C 101:35). The salt of the earth are those who enter the "everlasting gospel and covenant with an everlasting covenant" (D&C 101:39). They live the gospel to its fullest and dedicate their lives wholeheartedly to serving the Lord.

These "salt of the earth" saints are the rank and file of the Lord's Church. They are the people who daily staff the temples, the welfare facilities, and the missions of the Church. They are the members who greet everyone with a smile on Sundays. They are the members we can always count on to do their home and visiting teaching or to teach primary, nursery, and scouts. They are the people who teach lessons at the last minute when the assigned teacher doesn't show up. They don't worry about what callings they have, only about fulfilling those callings to the best of their ability and making a difference in the lives of the people they serve.

I learned a lesson years ago about the salt of the earth, but I have only more recently understood the importance of that lesson. I had been serving as an interim elders quorum president at BYU and was about to get married and leave the singles ward. The bishop of the ward asked for ideas about who I thought would make a solid replacement as the elders quorum president. When I gave my response without any hesitation, he was visibly surprised. Like every ward I had seen at BYU, our ward was filled with very intelligent, eloquent, and generally sharp people. But the name I gave did not belong to a particularly dynamic or flashy person.

However, as I explained to the bishop, the man I named was possibly the most dependable person in the quorum. Whenever we needed something done, we could count on him without even thinking twice. His chance to serve might have been missed because he was not among the most outwardly polished people, but I knew that he would do a good job because he was definitely among the most dependable.

In the years since that experience, I have realized that the vast majority of the Lord's work on earth is done by the rank and file, the dependable, the salt of the earth—not necessarily the sharpest or most eloquent members. This salt of the earth kind of person is exactly what the Lord needs to further His purposes on earth. This is at least in part what it means to become the salt of the earth. But this is only part of the Lord's teaching about the salt of the earth.

Salt Losing Its Savor

"But if the salt have lost his savour, wherewith shall it be salted? it is thenceforth good for nothing, but to be cast out, and to be trodden under foot of men" (Matthew 5:13). How, then, does salt lose its savor? Age does not affect salt. The salt in the oceans may well be as old as the oceans themselves. Likewise, salt cannot be chemically broken down. If it were, it would no longer be salt. Elder Carlos E. Asay noted the only ways that salt loses its savor. "A world-renowned chemist told me that salt will not lose its savor with age. Savor is lost through mixture and contamination."[3]

This is a lesson on keeping ourselves pure and on keeping our covenants. When we break the covenants that allow us to become the salt of the earth, we usually do so by contaminating ourselves with impurities of the world. If we allow this contamination, we risk becoming "good for nothing, but to be cast out, and to be trodden under foot of men" (Matthew 5:13).

Salt in Sacrifice and Covenant

In addition to salt's indispensable role as a preservative and seasoning, it was also linked with sacrifice and covenant. Of all the ways used in the scriptures to symbolically enter into covenant, *Smith's Bible Dictionary* lists eating salt as "more common and above all others."[4] On this same note, the Old Testament teaches, "And every oblation of thy meat offering shalt thou season with salt; neither shalt thou suffer the salt of the covenant of thy God to be lacking from thy meat offering: with all thine offerings thou shalt offer salt" (Leviticus 2:13). Numbers 18:19 and 2 Chronicles 13:5 also teach of a "covenant of salt." Likewise, in Ezekiel 43:24, the Lord also instructs His servants to "cast salt upon" the sacrifice.

Why would salt be eaten as a token of covenant? It is covenants that allow us to become the salt of the earth, and it is steadfastly keeping those covenants that makes us incorruptible, like salt. Here again we see the link between covenant and sacrifice. The principles of covenant and sacrifice allow us to take full advantage of the Atonement, the great and eternal sacrifice of the Son of God. As with every aspect of the Mosaic law, salt, as a part of sacrifice and covenant, was meant to draw us to Christ, that through His sacrifice we might be the salt of the earth if we enter into covenant with Him by taking upon ourselves His name.

Structure of Salt

Salt is a very unique compound, formed by the bonding of sodium and chlorine atoms. Its bond is ionic, or one in which the atoms share electrons in the outer shell (where the electrons orbit). Sodium contributes one electron, and chlorine contributes seven. Without this sharing, sodium remains sodium and chlorine remains chlorine. When the two combine, however, the useful compound of salt is formed.

Salt's molecular structure is a model of exactness. It always breaks

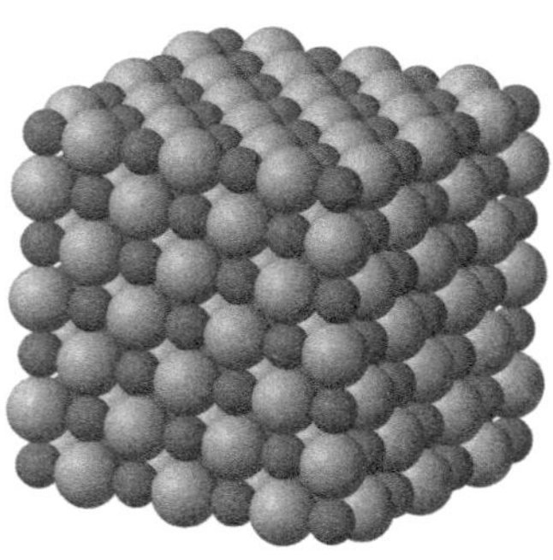

down into perfect cubes. From this cube, the symbol of the square, itself representing exactness, can be drawn from any one of the corners or edges.

In this respect, the cube is even more perfect than the square. This kind of exactness is the model for our obedience to the laws and ordinances of the gospel (see Alma 57:21). This exact obedience (read also: dependability) is key to becoming the salt of the earth.

Negative Applications of Salt

Like fire or light, salt also has negative or harmful applications in reality. Quite simply, the salt of the earth is not meant to be stagnant. It is meant to remain active and give constantly. Bodies of water that do not spring into rivers accumulate salt and become "good for nothing." If a body of water does not give or share a part of itself with the rest of the world, it cannot support life. The appropriately named "Dead Sea" earned its title because it has no outlet. The salt accumulates, and the sea supports no real life beyond brine shrimp. Its water is anything but refreshing because of its extremely high salt concentration.

Another example of stagnant salt causing problems comes from one of the most famous examples of wretched sin in society's history. Most archaeologists and scholars agree that Sodom, a city forever notorious for acting contrary to covenant, is covered up by what is now the south end of the Dead Sea.[5] Like the Sea that now covers it, Sodom could certainly be described as dead. Perhaps the near proximity of the Great Salt Lake, a North American Dead Sea, to the Church's headquarters in Salt Lake City should serve as a reminder to the Latter-day Saints of the importance of honoring covenants and continually flowing.

As illustrated by these examples, the salt of the earth is meant to flow with rivers. It is not meant to sit around doing nothing but to remain active and vibrant, anxiously engaged in a good cause (see D&C 58:27).

Notes

1. Carlos E. Asay, "Salt of the Earth: Savor of Men and Saviors of Men," *Ensign*, May, 1980, 42.
2. McConkie & Parry, *A Guide to Scriptural Symbols*, 96.
3. Carlos E. Asay, "Salt of the Earth," 42.
4. *Smith's Bible Dictionary*, 64.
5. Henry H. Halley, *Halley's Bible Handbook: An Abbreviated Bible Commentary* (Grand Rapids, MI: Zondervan, 1961), 98–99.

Blood

Blood is a prominent scriptural symbol that carries many diverse and seemingly contradictory meanings. In some scriptures, it represents the iniquity and impurity that stain the hands of a sinner. Isaiah wrote, "For your hands are defiled with blood, and your fingers with iniquity" (Isaiah 59:3). Likewise, Micah wrote, "They build up Zion with blood, and Jerusalem with iniquity" (Micah 3:10). In other scriptures, blood represents the exact opposite—not a stain or an impurity, but a washing and cleansing agent. Nephi recorded, "And these twelve ministers whom thou beholdest shall judge thy seed. And, behold, they are righteous forever; for because of their faith in the Lamb of God their garments are made white in his blood" (1 Nephi 12:10). John the Revelator also wrote, "And from Jesus Christ, who is the faithful witness, and the first begotten of the dead, and the prince of the kings of the earth. Unto him that loved us, and washed us from our sins in his own blood" (Revelation 1:5).

Sometimes, blood is an emblem of life. Jesus taught symbolically, "Except ye eat the flesh of the Son of man, and drink his blood, ye have no life in you. Whoso eateth my flesh, and drinketh my blood, hath eternal life" (John 6:53–54). This teaching was foreshadowed in the Old Testament, where it is taught that "the life of the flesh is in the blood" (Leviticus 17:11) and that "blood is the life" (Deuteronomy 12:23).

Yet in other scriptures, blood is an emblem of death. When Cain murdered Abel, the Lord confronted him, asking, "What hast thou done? the voice of thy brother's blood crieth unto me from the ground" (Genesis 4:10). When the Lord cursed Egypt through Moses, the river turned to blood, leading to death and stench (see Exodus 4:9; 7:20–21). However soon after this curse, many firstborn children were spared because the Israelites had smeared blood over their "side posts and upper door post" (Exodus 12:7, 13).

How can one emblem represent so many contradictory things? Because of its multiple and seemingly paradoxical meanings, blood is much like the tree of knowledge of good and evil. It represents life, yet it also is associated with death. It represents an action contrary to the commandments of God, yet it is still very much a holy and beneficial thing for all of mankind. The key to understanding the apparent paradox of the Fall and the tree of knowledge of good and evil is to understand its relationship with the tree of life. Likewise, with blood, the key to understanding and harmonizing its symbolic import is also to look to the symbolic tree of life: the Savior and His Atonement. As blood is inseparable with sacrifice, it is likewise inseparable with the sacrifice of the Lamb of God.

SACRIFICE

In Matthew 19, the Savior responded to a young man who had asked what was required to gain eternal life. The Savior's answer may seem simple on the surface, but there is a great deal to be learned from His words and the order in which the Savior listed the commandments. "Thou shalt do no murder, Thou shalt not commit adultery, Thou shalt not steal, Thou shalt not bear false witness, Honour thy father and thy mother, and Thou shalt love thy neighbor as thyself" (Matthew 19:18–19).

In recounting the ten commandments, the Messiah began with the sixth and ended with the fifth (the tenth commandment was not mentioned verbally). The young man replied that he had lived in compliance with these commandments. Christ then replied, "If thou wilt be perfect, go and sell that thou hast, and give to the poor, and thou shalt have treasure in heaven: and come and follow me" (Matthew 19:21). This invitation was not as well received, as the young man walked away unwilling to make such a sacrifice of his worldly possessions (see Matthew 19:22).

From this we learn two principles that are absolutely central to the Atonement and plan of salvation: sacrifice and obedience. With the exception of the fifth commandment, the commandments listed by the Savior were "thou shalt nots"—the practices to be avoided. We may gain some insight into why the Savior listed these by noting His final invitation to the young man. "If thou wilt be perfect, go and sell that thou hast, and give to the poor." This is a commandment of sacrifice. The first four commandments that were not mentioned by the Savior can be considered commandments of sacrifice in that they are all dealing directly with God and putting Him directly ahead of anything else (i.e., no other gods, no graven images, and so forth). Could it be that Christ did not mention the commandments of sacrifice, which could be simply defined as trading things of man for things of God, because He knew that the young man was unwilling to obey such commandments?

Obedience

The commandments that the Savior listed are also commandments of obedience—things we are commanded to do or not to do. After inviting the young man to sacrifice his worldly possessions, the Savior taught this concept of obedience by bidding the young man, "come and follow me" (Matthew 19:21). Is there anywhere a more direct invitation to obey than this?

The commandments, and this story of their application, teach us that in order to receive a celestial reward ("eternal life" in the young man's case) we must follow a celestial pattern, one marked by sacrifice and obedience.

To understand the principle of obedience fully, we must understand the doctrine of the Fall of Adam. We know that Adam and Eve were commanded not to partake of the forbidden fruit (see Genesis 2:17). Yet we also know that they did partake of the fruit and, as a result, were cast out of the Garden of Eden, or out of the presence of God (see Genesis 3:23). This act introduced both disobedience and mortality into the world. Man was banished from the presence of Deity and left to learn, grow, and age. Death, both physical and spiritual, came as a result of the Fall. Disobedience brought death from that time, just as obedience brings life. "For as in Adam all die, even so in Christ shall all be made alive" (1 Corinthians 15:22).

The death brought on by disobedience is quite literal. To bring this point closer to home, consider the two major causes of death in America: heart disease and cancer. What are they in essence? They are disobedience.

They are a heart ceasing to function they way it was designed to function and cells behaving out of control. They are nothing more or less than living things not behaving the way they were intended and designed, and that is the essence of disobedience. Think of it—if everything were completely obedient, the heart would never stop beating, blood would never leave its path, skin would never sag or be torn, hair would never fall out or turn grey. All elements in obedience would react perfectly. Quite simply, we would never die.

Perfection and obedience are so closely connected that perfection comes through obedience and only through obedience. Of course, perfection could not exist in mortality. And that is precisely the point! Perfection is an immortal or eternal concept, not a mortal or temporal one. With the Fall of Adam came mortality. With mortality came disobedience, and with disobedience came death. Death and the physical effects of aging are personal extensions of the Fall, felt by all the descendants of Adam. Imperfection and disobedience are two of the hallmarks of mortality, brought on by the Fall. In another part of the Garden of Eden, the tree of life stood. This tree can now only be reached by obedience, which leads to perfection, the hallmark of immortality and eternal life.

As death is the consequence of disobedience and the Fall, a way has been provided that we might gain divine help and thereby overcome these deaths and move toward eternal life and the tree of life. This way is through sacrifice. King Benjamin taught about the connection between the principles of sacrifice and obedience. "For the natural man is an enemy to God, and has been from the fall of Adam, and will be forever and ever, unless he yields to the enticings of the Holy Spirit, and putteth off the natural man and becometh a saint through the atonement of Christ the Lord, and becometh as a child, submissive, meek, humble, patient, full of love, willing to submit to all things which the Lord seeth fit to inflict upon him, even as a child doth submit to his father" (Mosiah 3:19). The man of this world remains an enemy to God and is not fit for His kingdom unless he makes a sacrifice—unless he trades in his will for the will of God "even as a child doth submit to his father."

Notice the similarities between the concept of becoming as a child and submitting to the will of the Father and the fifth commandment that Christ taught in closing to the young man: "Honor thy father and mother" (Matthew 19:19). We honor our Heavenly Parents by making the sacrifice of submitting ourselves to their will. Like all sacrifices we may be asked to make, this sacrifice is a reminder and a type of the great and last sacrifice (see Alma 34:10). Not coincidentally, Adam and Eve offered animal sacrifices almost immediately after the Fall (see Moses 5:6).

BLOOD

Linking the principles of sacrifice and obedience is blood. Blood is also the link between mortality and immortality and between imperfection and perfection.

Blood was introduced into Adam and Eve's bodies as a result of their disobedience in partaking of the forbidden fruit, as such it became a token and direct result of disobedience. Joseph Smith taught that blood is notably absent from a resurrected or incorruptible body, which we could also call a perfectly obedient body.[1] Therefore, blood goes hand in hand with the Fall and the tree of knowledge of good and evil in that blood is a representation of both life and death. Quite simply, blood is the representation of mortality.

All Old Testament sacrifices were centered around the shedding of blood as a similitude of the great and ultimate sacrifice of the Lamb of God. "For the life of the flesh is in the blood: and I have given it to you upon the altar to make an atonement for your souls: for it is the blood that maketh an atonement for the soul" (Leviticus 17:11). John further clarified this point. "But if we walk in the light, as he is in the light, we have fellowship one with another, and the blood of Jesus Christ his Son cleanseth us from all sin" (1 John 1:7).

Paul taught the Hebrews—the very people who had been practicing the sacrificial rites of the Mosaic law for generations—exactly why they had been commanded to offer those sacrifices. "And almost all things are by the law purged with blood; and without shedding of blood is no remission" (Hebrews 9:22).

As part of this law, once a year, the high priest would enter the Holy of Holies and sprinkle the blood of a sacrifice on the mercy seat (see Hebrews 9:7, 12). As we discussed earlier, this sprinkling of blood was an obvious representation of the Atonement; it was even offered on Yom Kippur, the Day of Atonement. As Paul taught, "For the bodies of those [sacrificial] beasts, whose blood is brought into the sanctuary by the high priest for sin, are burned without the camp. Wherefore Jesus also, that he might sanctify the people with his own blood, suffered without the gate" (Hebrews 13:11–12).

It is clear that blood is an emblem of the Atonement, the ultimate sacrifice that makes perfection possible. Since the Atonement brings life, even eternal life, it is fitting that the Lord also chose blood as a token of the beginning of life, birth, along with water and the spirit (see Moses 6:59–60).

When we put together these pieces of what the Lord has taught us, it becomes clear why He chose blood as a token for the Atonement. Luke recounts for us the single most significant event since the Creation: "And he was withdrawn from them about a stone's cast, and kneeled down, and prayed, Saying, Father, if thou be willing, remove this cup from me: nevertheless not my will, but thine be done. And there appeared an angel unto him from heaven, strengthening him. And being in an agony he prayed more earnestly: and his sweat was as it were great drops of blood falling down to the ground" (Luke 22:41–44).

With the revelations of the restored gospel of Jesus Christ, we are better able to understand that through the Atonement the Savior took our sins upon Himself. He suffered not only for us but because of us. His blood paid the price for our sins, our shortcomings of mortality.

Again, what does blood represent? It is the element of this world, of mortality and of corruptibility. That is precisely what was sacrificed for our sins—the world! Mortality, sin, and disobedience were all traded in, all sacrificed, for obedience, purity, and immortality through the shedding of the Lamb's blood. By the complete purging of His blood, the Savior literally sacrificed mortality and worldliness for immortality and the kingdom of heaven.

Christ paid the debt for our shortcomings of mortality with the emblem of mortality itself. Our Lord asks the same thing of us—that we sacrifice our worldliness, our will as natural men and enemies to God, and that which is temporal for that which is eternal: the will of God and "treasure in heaven" (Matthew 19:21).

It is also noteworthy that Elder Bruce R. McConkie suggested that the angel who visited Christ (see Luke 22:43) was Michael or Adam, the one through whom mortality and blood first came.[2]

Family

There is one other representation of blood that cannot be ignored. In addition to its many other connotations and denotations, blood also represents family. Members of the restored Church become the "blood of Israel," meaning that they are part of the Lord's covenant people. They are family in a very real sense.

Fittingly, this is another benefit of the Atonement. Through it, we may become the children—the family—of Christ. "And now, because of the covenant which ye have made ye shall be called the children of Christ, his sons and his daughters; for behold, this day he hath spiritually begotten you; for ye say that your hearts are changed through faith on his name; therefore, ye are born of him and have become his sons and his daughters" (Mosiah 5:7).

Summary

There is a common saying among patriots and members of the military that "the price of freedom is blood." Sadly, history has proven this to be true in the physical sense. In fact, this may even be considered one of the central messages of the Book of Mormon. Learning the spiritual from the temporal, there is no question that the price of freedom—freedom from sin and captivity of the devil—is also blood, the blood of the Lamb of God.

Because of His infinite sacrifice, we are able to repent, put off the "natural man" of mortality, and be reconciled with God. It is only because of this sacrifice that obedience is of any benefit to us. Just as Christ taught the young man that obedience is profitable only when it is coupled with sacrifice, so it is with our own works—they are dead without the Atonement.

It is the Atonement that makes all blessings possible. Likewise, this Atonement, this great and last sacrifice, profits us nothing if we do not follow it with a sacrifice of our own, trading in our will for the will of God through making and honoring covenants and by living with strict obedience to the laws and ordinances of the gospel.

Notes

1. Joseph Smith, Jr., *Teachings of the Prophet Joseph Smith*, 367.
2. Bruce R. McConkie, "The Purifying Power of Gethsemane," *Ensign*, May 1985, 9.

Olives

Olives and their oil have taken on many interesting and important meanings in the scriptures. Generally speaking, olive oil represents the Holy Ghost.[1] The Doctrine and Covenants' interpretation of the parable of the ten virgins tells us that the five virgins whose lamps were filled with olive oil (see Matthew 25:1–13) were those who had filled their lives with the Holy Ghost. "And at that day, when I shall come in my glory, shall the parable be fulfilled which I spake concerning the ten virgins. For they that are wise and have received the truth, and have taken the Holy Spirit for their guide, and have not been deceived—verily I say unto you, they shall not be hewn down and cast into the fire, but shall abide the day" (D&C 45:56–57).

Uses of Olive Oil

Olive oil was used both internally and externally. It is still commonly used as a cooking oil. "It was often used as a poultice believed to drain infection or sickness. As an ointment, olive oil—mingled with other liquids—soothed bruises and wounds and open sores. (In Jesus' parable, oil and wine were poured by the Good Samaritan into the wounds of the robbed and beaten traveler near Jericho)."[2]

Olive oil was extremely useful and versatile, but these are only the beginning of the eternal applications and symbolic lessons it carries.

Fuel for Lamps

Understanding that oil represents most prominently the Holy Ghost or the Spirit of the Lord, it is no surprise that olive oil was the chief source of light in biblical times (besides, of course, the sun). "Thy word is a lamp unto my feet, and a light unto my path" (Psalms 119:105). Lamps give light so that we can see the path to follow. But the lamp won't give light without fuel. Again, oil from olives was the common fuel used in the Bible. This use of olive oil makes it a remarkably appropriate symbol for the Holy Ghost, which is our source of spiritual light and warmth. Understanding this symbolism of light and the Holy Ghost opens the door to the many roles that olive oil plays in scriptural symbolism.

Anointing

Since we live in a world of electricity and light bulbs, it is easy for us to overlook the importance that oil for lamps had anciently. Instead, we probably associate olive oil most closely with the concept of anointing. However, even this concept is skewed because we tend to associate anointing only with healing the sick. Anointing actually has many other uses, all of which are important to understand symbolically.

Anointing as Part of the Temple

Among many other things, anointing was performed as a part of the temple rites revealed in Exodus. First Aaron and his sons, as workers in the temple, were to be washed with water (see Exodus 29:4). This is what we refer to simply as washings. Then after being clothed ("to clothe" is one of the meanings of the Greek word *enduo*[3] from which the English word "endowment" comes), they were anointed with oil (see Exodus 29:7, 21). Remembering that oil represents the Holy Ghost, washing and anointing take us back to Christ's words to Nicodemus. "Except a man be born of water and of the Spirit, he cannot enter into the kingdom of God" (John 3:5).

We equate being born of water and the Spirit with baptism, and rightly so. However, here we see that rebirth of water and the Spirit also have their part in the rites of the temple, both anciently and in the restored gospel (see D&C 124:37–39). Washing and anointing are, in this sense, a birth of water and of the Spirit just like baptism. For we also know that without the temple, we can in no wise enter or even see the kingdom of God.

Anointing to Holy Offices

Anointing with oil was also a biblical practice for setting apart individuals to particular and high offices.

- Samuel used olive oil to anoint Saul as a "captain" over the Lord's inheritance (1 Samuel 10:1) and later as a king over Israel (see 1 Samuel 15:1).
- David was anointed as the king over Israel (see 2 Samuel 12:7).
- King Solomon was anointed a king with olive oil (see 1 Kings 1:39).
- Jehu was likewise anointed a king with olive oil (see 1 Kings 19:16).
- Elisha was anointed to a different office, that of a prophet (see 1 Kings 19:16).
- Aaron and his sons were anointed with olive oil as priests to preside in and enter the tabernacle (see Exodus 28:41).
- Even in modern times, monarchs such as Queen Elizabeth II have been initiated into their offices by being anointed with oil.[4]

In all these holy offices, followers of Christ are anointed with oil so that the Spirit of the Lord will be upon them in their sacred callings. With this Spirit, they are justified (see Moses 6:60) and properly prepared to serve the Lord.

However, the importance of olive oil does not end there. All of these holy offices are a type and shadow of the Savior. The Savior—the ultimate Prophet, Priest, and King—was anointed in all His divine capacities (see Isaiah 61:1; Luke 4:18; Acts 10:38). In one of Christ's first acts after His forty-day retreat to the wilderness, He entered a synagogue and read a scripture originally found in Isaiah. "The Spirit of the Lord is upon me, because he hath anointed me to preach the gospel to the poor; he hath sent me to heal the brokenhearted, to preach deliverance to the captives, and recovering of sight to the blind, to set at liberty them that are bruised" (Luke 4:18; Isaiah 61:1).

This scripture shows us again the connection between "the Spirit of the Lord" and anointing (as with oil). Moreover, the scripture teaches us that the Messiah had at last arrived. The Old Testament is full of prophecies of a Messiah, which in Hebrew literally means "the anointed."[5] The Greek word for the same is what we now know as Christ.[6] By proclaiming Himself as one "anointed" or the Messiah, the Jews thought Him guilty of blasphemy. Jesus is the Christ, the Messiah, the Anointed One of the Father. However, the Jews, in their hardness of heart, looked beyond the mark; they did not recognize their own King and even crucified Him (see Jacob 4:14).

Following the example of the Messiah, earthly ordinations of prophets, priests, and kings serve not just to hallow the individual for his or her calling, but to conform us to the image of the Messiah (see Romans 8:29).

Healing

Perhaps we most commonly associate the word "anoint" with another function of the priesthood: Administering to the sick and afflicted. This brings us to another scriptural function of oil. The disciples of Christ "cast out many devils, and anointed with oil many that were sick and healed them" (Mark 6:13). The brother of the Savior writes, "Is any sick among you? let him call for the elders of the church; and let them pray over him, anointing him with oil in the name of the Lord: And the prayer of faith shall save the sick, and the Lord shall raise him up; and if he have committed sins, they shall be forgiven him" (James 5:14–15).

The gifts of healing and being healed are gifts of the Spirit (see D&C 46:19–20). Therefore, they come as a function of the Holy Ghost (see D&C 46:11). Paul taught this anciently (see 1 Corinthians 12), and the same doctrine has been revealed as an integral part of the restored gospel (see D&C 46; Moroni 10). Keeping in mind the source of these blessings, anointing the sick or afflicted with oil is a symbolic representation of the Spirit of the Lord being given to those who suffer.

Olive Oil in Sacrifices

The application of olive oil in healing becomes even more apparent when we view oil in the context of the principle of sacrifice. Leviticus 2:4 names an offering of baked meat to be brought forth along with "unleavened cakes of fine flour mingled with oil, or unleavened wafers anointed with oil." Oil is also used numerous other times as a dressing for and a part of sacrifices in the temple.

Notice the symbolic connection between healing, sacrifice, and oil. Christ is the great healer. He is the "Sun of righteousness" with "healing in his wings" (Malachi 4:2). This healing is also symbolic of the great and last sacrifice: the Atonement. As Isaiah poetically wrote, "Surely he hath borne our griefs, and carried our sorrows: yet we did esteem him stricken, smitten of God, and afflicted. But he was wounded for our transgressions, he was bruised for our iniquities: the chastisement of our peace was upon him; and with his stripes we are healed" (Isaiah 53:4–5). His stripes—His afflictions and sacrifice—are the mode by which all healing ultimately takes place. Oil, as shown by the scriptures mentioned, is also inseparably connected with the healing that comes through the Savior by way of His sacrifice.

When we understand that these principles are inseparable, even the blessings of healing that come through the Holy Ghost are, in this sense, a type and a foreshadowing of the eternal healing that comes through the Atonement.

The Olive Press

That Atonement that makes all eternal healing possible was wrought in Gethsemane. Gethsemane being interpreted means "oil press."[7] This is understood as a reference to olives, as their oil was the precious oil, treasured in biblical times.[8] Olives were often pressed by large, solid, round rocks, which crushed the oil out of them. In Gethsemane, the weight of the sins of the world had a similar effect on the Savior; it literally crushed the atoning blood from every pore of His body (see Mosiah 3:7; D&C 19:18).

Job remarked, "I washed my steps with butter, and the rock poured me out rivers of oil" (Job 29:6). Understanding the rock as the Savior and oil as a symbol of the Holy Ghost, Job was summarizing the effects of the Atonement. The Rock—in the olive press of Gethsemane—poured out rivers of not just blood but also oil, or the Spirit. The healing power of His Atonement flowed from the appropriately named oil press.

According to at least one source, olive oil is also an antidote against serpent venom.[9] It was used by the Hebrews to literally counteract the poisonous venom of serpents.[10] We know that Lucifer is appropriately called the "serpent" (Revelation 12:9; 20:2) and that he appeared to Eve in the form of a serpent to tempt her (see Genesis 3:1). The Atonement wrought in the olive press of Gethsemane is certainly the antidote to this serpent's venom.

The Sacrament

In remembrance of this eternal sacrifice in Gethsemane, the Master instituted the ordinance of the sacrament. As we partake of the bread and water, which represent our Savior's body and blood, we evidence to God that we are willing to take on certain attributes and responsibilities. First, in connection with the bread, we state that we are willing to take upon ourselves the name of Christ, always remember Him, and keep the commandments which we have received by way of Him. More specific to the water, we witness that we do always remember Him and keep His commandments. In both cases, if we do these things we are promised the blessing of always having the Spirit with us (see Moroni 4:1–3; Moroni 5:1–2; D&C 20:77, 79).

In the sacrifice commemorated by the sacrament, the rock of the olive press (Gethsemane) gave forth its oil. Through the sacrament itself, the Rock, who is Christ, sheds forth His Spirit on those who do as He has invited.

The Olive Tree

The olive tree itself is particularly meaningful. One legend has it that the tree of life in the Garden of Eden was an olive tree.[11] The doors to the Temple of Solomon were carved out of the wood of an olive tree (see 1 Kings 6:31–33). Of all the trees that would have surrounded the Savior in His native land, the olive tree would have been the most prominent. It thrives in stony places, meaning it likes rocks. It bears fruit in its seventh year, a number commonly associated with perfection and completeness. Its yield becomes full in the fifteenth year. It then continues to bear fruit for the rest of its existence, which is usually hundreds of years.[12]

Section 88 of the Doctrine and Covenants was called by Joseph Smith the "olive leaf . . . plucked from the Tree of Paradise, the Lord's message of peace to us" (D&C 88—chapter heading). The olive leaf and branch have long been a symbol of peace, but from this section we learn that the olive leaf comes from the "Tree of Paradise." This "Tree of Paradise" would most certainly be a tree of peace, as peace is the message of the Savior and His Atonement, and He is "The Prince of Peace" (Isaiah 9:6). It is appropriate that what has been called the greatest sermon ever given was given on the Mount of Olives by the Prince of Peace. That same Mount of Olives is the spot from which He ascended into heaven (see Acts 1:9–12).

The olive tree is also used in the Book of Mormon as a representation of the Lord's covenant people, the House of Israel (see 1 Nephi 10:12; 15:12; Jacob 5–6), and Paul made a similar comparison in Romans 11. We have discussed that trees are often used as symbols of righteous people, but what would be so particular about olive trees that would draw this comparison with the House of Israel? Perhaps the answer lies with the Savior's teachings that "by their fruits ye shall know them" (Matthew 7:20). With olive oil representing the Holy Ghost, perhaps the olive tree represents the Spirit of the Lord being upon the House of Israel. The works of Israel are intended to be righteousness and an accompanying outpouring of the Spirit.

The olive tree comparison may also be a reference to the oil press of Gethsemane. We enter the House of Israel by making covenants. Likewise, we apply the Atonement—the healing oil of the olive press in Gethsemane—by making and keeping covenants. In this sense, the oil of the olive tree is the same fruit brought forth by the House of Israel.

SUMMARY

The Lord has beautifully and appropriately chosen olives, their oil, and their trees to represent many great and marvelous blessings. Olives are peace. They bring healing, especially from the diabolical venom of the serpent. They are part of the coronation of priests, kings, and prophets. They bring flavor to our food. Perhaps above all, they bring light. All of this is possible thanks to another role they play—the role of sacrifice, and most particularly the sacrifice in the oil press that was Gethsemane.

NOTES

1. McConkie & Parry, *A Guide to Scriptural Symbols*, 88.
2. Truman G. Madsen, "The Olive Press," *Ensign*, Dec. 1982, 57.

3. Strong, *Strong's Exhaustive Concordance of the Bible,* Greek word 1746.
4. The anointing portion of Queen Elizabeth's 1953 coronation ceremony is as follows:

   The Queen shall sit down in King Edward's Chair (placed in the midst of the Area over against the Altar, with a faldstool before it), wherein she is to be anointed. Four Knights of the Garter shall hold a rich pall of silk, or cloth of gold: the Dean of Westminster, taking the Ampulla and Spoon from off the Altar, shall hold them ready, pouring some holy Oil into the Spoon, and with it the Archbishop shall anoint the Queen in the form of a cross:

   On the palms of both hands, saying, Be thy Hands anointed with holy Oil.

   On the breast, saying, Be thy Breast anointed with holy Oil.

   On the crown of the head, saying, Be thy Head anointed with holy Oil: As kings, priests, and prophets were anointed:

   And as Solomon was anointed king by Zadok the priest and Nathan the prophet, so be thou anointed, blessed, and consecrated Queen over the Peoples, whom the Lord thy God hath given thee to rule and govern, In the name of the Father, and of the Son, and of the Holy Ghost. Amen.

   From http://www.oremus.org/liturgy/coronation/cor1953b.html.
5. Strong, *Strong's Exhaustive Concordance of the Bible,* Hebrew word 4899.
6. Ibid., Greek word 5547.
7. Ibid., Greek word 1068.
8. Madsen, "The Olive Press," 57.
9. Miles Martindale, *Dictionary of the Bible*, (New York: N. Bangs and T. Mason, 1823), 534.
10. Ibid.
11. Madsen, "The Olive Press," 57.
12. *Smith's Bible Dictionary*, 224.

Conclusion

The Lord has given us the temporal world not just for our enjoyment, but to teach us of the eternal. So many divine lessons can never and will never be learned if we do not learn this language of symbolism in order to learn the eternal from the temporal. Again, all temporal things given by the hand of God are designed to teach eternal lessons of the Savior and His gospel (see Moses 6:63; 2 Nephi 2:11). Even temporal works such as the Savior's miracles are meant to teach greater eternal and spiritual lessons. When we access the physical blessings of the Lord through something like a priesthood blessing with consecrated olive oil, the Savior's hope is that these blessings will lead us to greater eternal blessings from the Atonement. Likewise, as we are washed physically and temporally with water, the Savior's hope is that we will be washed spiritually and eternally through the Atonement.

When the Savior inquired, "What think ye of Christ? whose son is he?" the Pharisees answered, "The Son of David" (Matthew 22:42). This was true in the physical sense, as Christ was a descendant of David, but there is so very much more to Jehovah's divine Sonship. The Master responded,

> He saith unto them, How then doth David in spirit call him Lord, saying,
>
> The Lord said unto my Lord, Sit thou on my right hand, till I make thine enemies thy footstool?
>
> If David then call him Lord, how is he his son?
>
> And no man was able to answer him a word, neither durst any man

from that day forth ask him any more questions. (Matthew 22:43–46)

Yes, Christ is a son of David, in a physical sense. But even David calls Jesus "Lord" because He truly is the Son of God, not just physically, but spiritually also. The Pharisees and others never looked beyond the physical or the temporal, so they never recognized Jesus as the Son of God in either a physical or spiritual sense. They never discovered the true and matchless majesty of the Messiah.

All things truly do point to Christ. Physical symbols throughout the scriptures and the creations of God serve to point us to Christ and teach us of His divine role in the plan of salvation. There is so very much to learn about our Savior, our Father's divine plan, and what we need to do to take advantage of that plan. Our goal is to know our Father in Heaven and Jesus Christ (see John 17:3). We should be ever thankful that our loving Father has given us all things in this world to point us to Christ so that we can know to which source we may look for a remission of our sins (see 2 Nephi 25:26) and so that we can come to know our Lord and Savior.

Our challenge is not really to discover all the ways in which things of this world typify Christ. That is a very rewarding pursuit, and it certainly may help us learn about our Lord and what we must do to put His Atonement into effect in our lives, but it is not the full purpose of the scriptures, the creations of God, or gospel symbolism itself. Our true challenge in mortality is perhaps best expressed in the simple but beautiful primary song, "I Am a Child of God." In it, we sing, "Lead me, guide me, walk beside me. Help me find the way. Teach me all that I must do to live with him some day."[1]

Eternal life is not a matter of knowing facts; it is a matter of knowing God. To know God, which is more than just knowing about God, we must do His will. We must keep His commandments. We must walk before Him honoring high and holy covenants. That is the true purpose of the gospel and the symbols within it. I hope that these observations have served to express that divine truth. Although the observations in this book are somewhat deep and complicated, their purpose is beautifully simple. When all is said and done, the key to the gospel of Jesus Christ is very simple: keep the commandments.

Keeping the commandments will lead us to also become models or types of Christ, just like Adam, Joseph, Abraham, and Isaac. As Bruce R. McConkie said, "God grant that all of us may walk in the light as God our Father is in the light so that, according to the promises, the blood of Jesus Christ His Son will cleanse us from all sin."[2]

Notes

1. *Hymns*, no. 301.
2. McConkie, "The Purifying Power of Gethsemane," 9.

Amen

Along with the name of Jesus Christ, the proper conclusion for personal, public, or ordinance-related prayers; public church speeches; and testimonies (if not this book) is "amen." According to Webster's *amen* is "used after a prayer or to express approval."

Amen comes to us in English from Latin, Greek, and Hebrew. In Hebrew it carries the meanings "firm" and "true"[1] and is expressed in adverb form by the word "verily."[2] In English it most correctly means "so be it."

Amen is thus used "as a seal to the document of the supplication, attesting its genuineness as the true expression of the suppliant's soul; gathering within the compass of a word the meaning of all that has been uttered or thought."[3]

How does this point to Christ? In Revelation 3:14, *Amen* is given as one of the names of the Savior. Borrowing from Elder Talmage, Christ is the Word within whose compass the meaning of all that is good is gathered.

Notes

1. LDS Bible Dictionary, 607.
2. *Smith's Bible Dictionary*, 15.
3. Talmage, *Jesus the Christ*, 241–42.

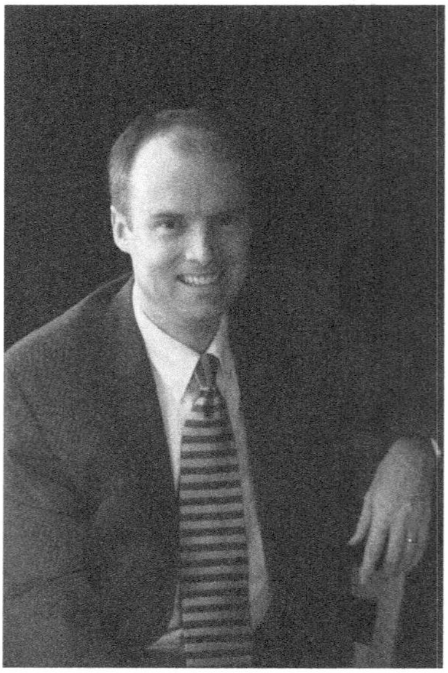

About the Author

Mark Shields has been happily married to his wife, the former Cami Chamberlain, since 1992. They are the proud parents of five daughters: Heidi, Kayla, Claire, Anna, and Robyn. He is currently serving as bishop of his ward in Mesa, Arizona. In the past he has served as an instructor for many temple preparation classes, missionary preparation classes, missionary training center classes, Primary and nursery classes, and Gospel Doctrine and Gospel Essentials classes. He has also served as a high councilor, a seminary teacher, and a temple worker.

Mark's first book *Your Endowment* discusses how to improve your temple worship. It was published in 2009.

Photograph by Jennifer Hughes

0 26575 52699 8